How to Change Anybody

ALSO BY DAVID J. LIEBERMAN, PH.D.

Make Peace with Anyone
Get Anyone to Do Anything
Never Be Lied to Again
Instant Analysis

How to
Change
Anybody

*Proven Techniques to Reshape
Anyone's Attitude, Behavior,
Feelings, or Beliefs*

DAVID J. LIEBERMAN, Ph.D.

St. Martin's Press ❧ New York

www.stmartins.com

Book design by Mary A. Wirth

ISBN 0-312-32474-X
EAN 978-0312-32474-2

First Edition: February 2005

10   9   8   7   6   5   4   3   2   1

Contents

I. How to Change Anyone's Beliefs and Values

Learn psychological strategies to eliminate anyone's unhealthy beliefs about anyone or anything and to realign their values in any area of life.

II. How to Change Anyone's Emotional State

Turn the unhappy into the happy and the neurotic into the normal, and make anyone feel emotionally stable, happier, and balanced. Whether it is your patient, parent, friend, or spouse, permanently shift anyone's state for the better.

III.   Plastic Surgery for the Personality

Discover the psychological principles that can rechannel a person's personality, nature, and character. Turn that annoying, arrogant, lazy, self-centered, self-absorbed person into a giving, kind, and easygoing pleasure.

IV.   How to Change Anyone's Attitude and Behavior

Use the power of psychology to rid anyone of a negative attitude about anything and eliminate any unwanted behavior. Whether it is your patient, child, friend, or spouse, help someone who doesn't want to, or thinks he doesn't need to, change—fast and for good.

Acknowledgments

Many hardworking, passionate, and dedicated people are involved in the process and ultimate success of any book. My thanks and appreciation go to my agent, Ian Klienert at The Literary Group. He is a consummate professional and a pleasure to work with. To my editor, Jennifer Enderlin at St. Martin's Press, who is a real talent, my gratitude for your terrific insights and suggestions. To my copy editor, Patricia Phelan, and production editor Meryl Gross, a big thank you. Their hard work is evident throughout the entire book. To John Karle, my extraordinary publicist, and to the great sales force at St. Martin's who have worked tirelessly on our previous books, thank you very much for an ongoing, outstanding job.

And most notably, my warmest thanks to those readers who have enjoyed my previous books, your kind letters of appreciation fuel my quest to continue writing books that try, in some small way, to enrich our lives.

Introduction

Don't let crazy people drive you crazy. Don't let annoying, petty, obnoxious individuals get under your skin. Why be annoyed and frustrated by those who don't listen to you, respect you, or care about you and what you want? Whether it's your child, spouse, friend, client, patient, boss, or coworker, why just "deal" with people when you can change them?

How to Change Anybody gives you the psychological tools to reshape and remake anyone into a better person. It shows you how to make permanent changes, not merely how to put up with difficult people or to be more tolerant.

Before you break up with your boyfriend, fire your employee, or write off your mother-in-law, change them into someone new. Why be contorted, twisting and turning yourself trying to accommodate others, when you can go right to the root of the problem—their beliefs, values, attitudes, or personality—and change it, fast and forever.

Who in your life could use a mental makeover, a little plastic surgery for the personality? Whether you don't like an employee's attitude, want a patient to quit drinking, wish your spouse would care more about appearance, want your mother-in-law to see the best in you, wish your friend would get out of an abusive relationship, or want your child to be more assertive, this book will show you how to achieve the change you desire, step-by-step. Armed with the psychological secrets governing human behavior, you will learn how to change anyone for the better—and to change *your* life for good.

A Note to the Reader

The techniques in *How to Change Anybody* are designed to change any and all aspects of a person. When we speak of change, however, we are not talking about turning someone into a slave to do your unconditional bidding. These psychological strategies work only to change someone *for the better.*

As you follow the advice in this book, you will discover that making real and permanent change in a person increases his or her sense of self-worth. So the techniques won't work unless the change you want to initiate is in the person's best interest. And when you want to help someone become a better person, you will find that you can change anybody faster and easier than you ever thought possible.

How to Use This Book

This book is designed to be used right away. You do not have to read any of the psychology involved if you do not want to, nor do you have to read the chapters that do not apply to your situation. To get started, look in the table of contents for the type of change you want to make and go right to the relevant chapter. There you will find step-by-step techniques that illustrate what to do and how to do it.

What If I Can't Find an Example of What I Want to Change?

A broad spectrum of examples are presented to illustrate the various types of psychological techniques. However, if you don't find the exact attitude or behavior you want to change, that's okay. Just apply the technique that is most similar to the type of change you want to make in someone.

Do I Have to Use All the Techniques in the Chapter?

Absolutely not. The psychological strategies are designed so you can select just a few from those offered, and still achieve success. Choose the simplest, fastest, and easiest techniques for your situation, based on the type of relationship, the time you're willing to invest, and the nature of the change you wish to make.

Some techniques do not require any significant investment of energy; they are noninvasive and can be used in most circumstances. Other strategies, however, require some degree of leverage over, and the cooperation of, the person. And of course, for more difficult people and situations, where there are serious issues—abuse, self-destructive behaviors, deep emotional problems, and so on—change usually requires a more comprehensive strategy, with more time, techniques, and leverage needed. In these instances the book shows what techniques are required and how to use them.

Can I Use Techniques from Other Sections?

The book is divided into four main sections, each representing an aspect of the human psyche. When required to effect change at a deeper level, we will gather in techniques from corresponding sections to round out your overall psychological strategy. Indeed, even something that seems uncomplicated, such as a wife hoping to make her husband more romantic, may require techniques aimed at more than just a behavioral change. For example, the man may have underlying values or beliefs that keep him from fully expressing himself.

And a seemingly topical change, such as having your sister care more about her appearance, cannot be achieved simply by dropping hints about losing weight, buying her a new wardrobe, or issuing ultimatums. You must see if she has conflicting values. For example, she may think, *If men think I'm attractive, they won't take me seriously.* Or she may have a belief built on a fear of intimacy, the attitude that people should just accept her as she is, or a pattern set in motion from childhood. So it's safe to say that putting a Diet Police magnet on the refrigerator is not going to get you too far.

Please note: Because these techniques are based on human nature, factors such as culture, race, and gender are either irrelevant or inconsequential.

How to Change Anyone's Beliefs and Values

Learn Psychological Strategies to Eliminate Anyone's Unhealthy Beliefs About Anyone or Anything and to Realign Their Values in Any Area of Life.

Man is what he believes.

—ANTON CHEKHOV

Chapter 1

Can You Change Someone Who Doesn't Want to Change?

Who wants to be a jerk? Who wants to have bad relationships, be sloppy, not care about anyone or anything but themselves, or pursue meaningless goals?

Everyone wants to be better. No one wants to engage in self-destructive behaviors. Nobody wants to be abusive, sustain a baseless hatred of others, have limited beliefs, be emotionally unstable, be obnoxious, and so on. None of these behaviors make us feel good. We want to change them, but we're unable to do so. We feel emotionally blocked from doing that which we know at some level is right for us and for our relationships.

Most people desperately want to change. We know this to be true in our own lives. When we are able to rise above our "baggage," we feel good about ourselves. Sure, there are people who say they are happy the way they are and don't want to change. But they are not being so truthful. Human beings are real pros at lying to themselves; in fact, it is when they lie most convincingly.

So can you change someone who doesn't want to change? The

question is irrelevant because this person does not really exist. All of us want to be better, to be fulfilled, and we are desperately seeking to use our potential and become something more. It is how we are made.

The psychological strategies presented in the following chapters allow you to navigate a way through a person's emotional blocks to create lasting change in almost any area. They allow you to make anyone a better person.

Chapter 2

Beliefs and Values: A Brief Introduction

To a large extent, beliefs and values are set in motion to justify our past, rationalize our current behavior, and make sense of events and circumstances in our lives.

Two types of values are *mean values* and *end values*. In order to accomplish an end value—happiness, for instance—a person places a priority on a mean value that will help him achieve his end objective.

For some this gateway to happiness may be money; for others, marriage and raising a family. Money becomes important because happiness is important, or family is important because happiness is important.

Now, if the underlying belief that connects the equation—this will give me that—is changed, then the mean value becomes unnecessary and it falls away. To change how a person feels about something, you reshape the belief that connects the two values. For instance, if a man believes money leads to happiness and then discovers that that is a false belief, his priorities change, as does his subsequent behavior.

Our psychological solution is to break down the belief, severing its emotional hold. For example, statistics show that there is a 90 percent likelihood that a woman who is highly promiscuous and who is engaged in rampant casual sex, prostitution, or both, was sexually abused as a girl or young adult. In order to make sense of what happened to her, she is forced, albeit unconsciously, to reduce the significance of the event. This is done by diluting the value and sanctity of sexual relations. Her willful promiscuity makes what happened to her less significant. So the value of what was harmed, of what was taken from her, has been reduced. Otherwise she would be forced to reconcile something much more traumatic. Therefore, she does what so many of us do, and takes the path of least resistance. Devaluing the sex act, diluting it to the point of insignificance, reinforces her belief that it doesn't matter.

Through a series of psychological techniques, you can change the unconscious calculation whereby it's simply easier on the psyche to believe differently, and so the person naturally chooses a different path. If you remove the *need* to hold on to a belief, no matter how deeply ingrained, the behavior attached to it melts away.

Chapter 3

Make Anyone More Moral and Ethical

Do you know someone whose moral compass is malfunctioning? If you are tired of someone's subhuman values, then it is possible for you to do something about it. Whether your daughter is sleeping around, a coworker is stealing office supplies, or your spouse is cheating at the weekly card game, you can use the following psychological techniques to instill a greater sense of morality in them.

Technique 1: The One-Million-Dollar Test

It's easy to believe in something if there is nothing at stake. Take, for example, a businessman who will not hire a minority to work for his company. If you were to tell the employer that this person can bring a million dollars into his business, the man now has a conflict and, therefore, must make a choice. Research shows that the best bet, statistically, is that he will hire this person. Therefore, the employer has to readjust his views of minorities; otherwise he has to consider himself a greedy fiend who sells his soul for money. It's much easier on his ego to conclude that maybe "they" aren't that bad. Either way, you begin to break down his belief system.

It's easy to have values when you don't have a conflict. Just like this businessman. But if you create a conflict—between what he believes and what he wants—you throw a monkey wrench into his thinking. In short, something has to give. Let's see how this works.

EXAMPLE: *Bill thinks it's okay to walk out of a restaurant without paying for the meal.*

What is Bill's belief? The restaurant didn't provide the service he deserved? Other people do it, too? The owner is a mean guy? They'll never miss his couple of bucks? Clearly these are rationalizations. If Bill thought about it, he'd realize that not paying the check is wrong—but he doesn't *want* to think about it.

Bill's wife introduces information that creates a conflict between Bill's belief and something that he wants. One of these will give. She says, "You know, Bill, little Jimmy is getting old enough to understand these things. And he thinks that if you do something, then it's okay for him to do it, too." Now the stakes have changed. The equation is no longer about a stolen meal without a guilty conscience. Rather it becomes, *Stolen meal = Corrupting son.* This conflict helps to change Bill's behavior in the short run, and in conjunction with the other techniques, he will in time come to reevaluate his belief.

SHAME ON YOU!

There is something to be said for attacking the ego head-on. If a woman is told that others know all about what she does, that they find her actions beneath her and are disgusted by them, she may adjust her behavior. For example, you tell her, "You know, a lot of people know about your cheating/stealing/lying, and they have known for some time. Everyone thinks you're great, but they are also put off by this." Although this may not result in a permanent change in her behavior, it may very well embarrass her into a short-term change.

Technique 2: Backdoor Consensus

Studies show that when we vocalize an opinion, whether or not we believe it to be true, in time we usually come to support it. For instance, in a class assignment, students were chosen randomly to take different sides of an issue. After mock debates, the students overwhelmingly accepted—or at least sympathized with—the position they had to defend, even when they did not initially believe it to be true.

EXAMPLE: *Parents of a promiscuous teenage girl want to put a stop to her behavior.*

The parents should have the girl speak with a younger sister, female relative, or neighbor about the importance of waiting until marriage or committing to one person. (A younger person is preferred because it puts the daughter in a position of responsibility and authority.) The parents can also arm their daughter with "talking points" by giving her readily available statistics showing, for example, that teens who sleep around have a higher rate of suicide, and drug and alcohol abuse. Ideally, these should be regular talks, and in time the message will begin to take root.

And if you want to, it is fine to give her some type of external reward—money, a special privilege, a present—as an incentive to speak with this other person. However, after the first few times, ask her to do it without any compensation. When she agrees, you'll know she's turned the psychological corner and has begun to embrace the very ideas you have been espousing.

(Note: If you believe that this person is the victim of past or current sexual abuse, professional help should be sought immediately.)

Technique 3: Image Consistency

When someone sees us in a flattering light, we often strive to maintain the image that he has of us. When others think well of us, it helps us to think better of ourselves, and so we are often unconsciously driven to not let them down.

Interestingly, the more fleeting the relationship the more we may try, because we do not have to sustain our efforts for very long. Do you know someone who would bend over backward to help a person he hardly knows, but when it comes to his family, he won't lift a finger? Did a friend of a friend or a distant relative ever comment that you were so nice, a great cook, very handy, and so forth? And did you then find yourself jumping through hoops in order to keep this image alive and well in regard to this person? Let's see how this works.

EXAMPLE: *Your friend Joan thinks it's okay to borrow things from your house and then forget to return them.*

In such a situation, say something like "You really know what it means to be a friend who respects other people's property. Like the time when you asked to borrow my car, even though the keys were in the ignition and you could have just taken it. I want you to know I really appreciate that about you." This should be enough to make Joan decide to ask permission before taking anything in the future. And anything that Joan already has of yours will likely be promptly returned. However, if this does not happen, that's fine. After an hour or so of applying the technique, simply ask her for it, and her willingness to comply will have increased tenfold.

The three simple sentences you say to Joan reshape the definition of your friendship to include someone who behaves with honesty and integrity. It makes Joan want to live up to the image you have of her, and she will be driven, mostly unconsciously, to fulfill your expectations. You see her in a certain light, and she seeks to protect this positive image.

THE ASCH EXPERIMENT

During this classic experiment, subjects were asked to find the best match for the line in box A from the lines in box B. When asked alone, almost every person chose the middle line. But when the subjects first listened to several other people, who were in on the experiment and who unanimously gave a wrong answer, 76 percent of the subjects gave the group's incorrect answer rather than trust their own judgment (Asch 1956). There was no pressure to conform, only the mere presence of others. Subsequent studies show that conformity and social pressure are strongest when the person does not have an ally, someone in his corner, agreeing with him. So for maximum advantage, when you use the psychological techniques in this book, make sure the person is not with someone whose own moral center is questionable.

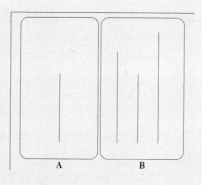

Technique 4: General Consensus

The great thinker Friedrich Nietzsche once mused, "Insanity in individuals is something rare, but in groups, parties, nations, and epochs, it is the rule." In Roman times infanticide was common and acceptable as, indeed, it remains today in certain parts of the world. While most people consider this practice abhorrent, when everyone is doing it, it becomes accepted. This is true for positive as well as negative behaviors.

Numerous studies show that even our character is greatly influenced by our environment. Municipalities understand that graffiti needs to be removed as quickly as possible, because as soon as any appears it creates a breeding ground for graffiti by others who previously thought it unacceptable. Another illustration is "mob mentality," the phenomenon where people in groups tend to support more extreme ideas than they would consider on an individual basis.

If everyone is on the "same page," an environment of expectations is created that is very powerful in shaping how we see ourselves. To raise people's moral consciousness, let them be part of a world where such appropriate behavior is the rule, not the exception.

Our identity is very much tied in with where we live, the people we know, and the places we go. By removing individuals from their environments, you shake up their self-concepts and make it easier for them to see themselves differently and, quite often, more objectively. You also get them away from the influences and triggers that snap them back into negative patterns.

EXAMPLE: *A girl thinks that it's okay to bully kids of other races.*

A girl who bullies children of other races should be removed from her environment and placed around individuals who have a higher sense of morality. How long she remains with them depends upon how much leverage you have and how ingrained the prejudice is. Even a weekend can help make a difference, though generally speaking, the longer she is exposed to an enlightening atmosphere, the more lasting the impact will be.

If the girl thinks that hurting people because they are of a certain race is okay, it is because of her influences. If you change the influences, you begin to change the girl.

Technique 5: Raising the Bar

Raising the bar is a fantastic technique that is very easy to do. Here, instead of chastising the person for a behavior, you lavish the person with praise and compliments. Then, after you are done with this five-minute emotional boost, you simply inform the person that the behavior you want corrected is unacceptable. In this way you fault the behavior, not the person.

EXAMPLE: *A teacher catches a student cheating on a test.*

The teacher calls the student into his office and says, "Julie, you are one of the brightest students I have ever had. Sometimes it comes through in tests, sometimes it doesn't, but I know what you are capable of. I also see how considerate you are of your classmates and how you are there for your friends. You have terrific potential, and I believe you can be and do anything that you want. You're the kind of girl who can achieve anything if you set your mind to it. I hope you'll remember to thank me for teaching you when you're a big success. Keep working hard, and strive to live your dreams. If anyone can, you can." Then almost as an afterthought, the teacher gently brings up the behavior: "Oh, I know most kids probably cheat on a test or two from time to time, but it's really beneath you. I'll see you tomorrow in class." This simple but powerful technique makes it nearly impossible for Julie to cheat on a test in this teacher's class again.

Strategy Review

- It's easy to maintain a belief when a person doesn't have anything at stake. Change the situation so that the person has more to lose by engaging in this corrupt behavior.
- Studies show that when we publicly express an idea — whether or not we believe it to be true — we usually come to support it.
- Reshape how people see themselves by letting them know that you believe them to be good and moral, and that *that* is precisely what you respect about them so much.
- If everyone is on the "same page," an environment of expectations is created that is very powerful in shaping how we see ourselves.
- Instead of chastising someone's bad behavior, lavish the person with praise, and then casually mention their misconduct as something that may be fine for others, but not for someone as terrific as the individual in question.

See These Chapters for Additional Strategies:

⇨ Chapter 5: **Eliminate Prejudice in Anyone**
⇨ Chapter 9: **The Gift of Self-Esteem**

Chapter 4

Inspire Loyalty in Anyone

What is it that makes a person stick by you in your darkest hour, while others run for the hills at the slightest hint that something is wrong? Are you tired of fair-weather friends who stab you in the back the minute you turn around? Whether it is a friend, employee, or spouse, you can make anyone more loyal to you, your company, or your cause. The following techniques contain the components, the building blocks, that make a person, any person, form an unshakable allegiance.

Technique 1: Bring Him in on the Inside

A person's loyalty is determined by which side of the fence he thinks he's on. Therefore, if you bring him to your side and make him part of your team, he will fight your battles with you, against the "other guys." To turn an outsider into an insider, you need to give him information that few people have, as well as some degree of power or authority within your organization or team.

EXAMPLE: *A sales manager has a salesperson whose loyalty is questionable.*

During a relaxed, private conversation, the sales manager should say something like, "Chris, I want you to know that there are going to be some changes around here. Mainly, we're close to acquiring the XYZ account, and we think you are the key person on the team to figure out how we can best service them. Now this is not public yet, so I need to count on your discretion."

It's amazing how quickly this technique helps to build allegiance. Now that Chris is a big shot, on the "inside" with a little bit of power, he won't be turning on his manager anytime soon.

Technique 2: A Part of Greatness

Studies show that the moods of sports fans are affected by the teams they support. When a football team wins, the fans feel great. But when the team loses, the fans feel worse. Moreover, *how* people identify with a team is fascinating. When their team wins, they say, "*Our* team won." But when they lose, they often say, "*They* lost." They give up their identification when things are not going smoothly.

We all want to be part of something great, to be with someone great, and to attach ourselves to a winner. To inspire loyalty, let others see the greatness within you, or what it is that you want them to believe in. You accomplish this by being the one who does what is right, even when an easier course of action is readily available.

EXAMPLE: *You want your friends and coworkers to be more loyal to you.*

Let's say you are playing a game of Trivial Pursuit with friends, and an argument ensues over whether another player's answer is right. If you believe it is, then voice your support for that player. In other words, take a position that is unfavorable to you.

Long after the game is forgotten, you will be known as the person who took the high road even though it was not in your best interest. People will seek you out and want to be a part of what you do. A principled person stands alone in the ability to command unwavering loyalty.

Technique 3: Little by Little

We all have a strong desire to stand by our convictions and to think of ourselves as someone who is consistent. When we flip-flop too much on things we say and do, we can feel less secure and confident. Research in this area illustrates how effective this psychological factor is when it is applied to instilling loyalty. For example, when people are presented with a small request and subsequently comply with it, they are much more likely to agree to a larger request as long as it is consistent with the smaller one. When they take a small step in one direction, people are driven to maintain a sense of consistency by agreeing to larger requests. Simply, those who agree to a smaller request reshape their attitude and beliefs to include the definition that they are individuals who support this idea. Therefore, agreeing to the larger request is just doing something for a cause that they already firmly "believe" in.

RESEARCH IN ACTION

Freedman and Fraser (1966) asked homeowners to let them place a huge Drive Carefully sign in their front yards. Only 17 percent gave permission. Other residents, however, were approached with a smaller request. Asked to put up a three-inch Be A Safe Driver window sign, nearly all immediately agreed. A few weeks later, these homeowners were asked to place the gigantic Drive Carefully sign on their front lawns. This group—76 percent consented—overwhelmingly agreed. Called the "foot-in-the-door technique," this study demonstrates the tendency for people who have first agreed to a small request to comply later with a larger one.

EXAMPLE: *You want customers to be more loyal to you and your company.*

To instill loyalty in customers, invite them to the company picnic; have them speak to, and get to know, your employees; ask them for references, referrals, suggestions on how you can improve your business relationship. (These little steps build internal momentum and are effective for establishing loyalty in anyone.) Clearly such customers *must* care about your company because they have invested themselves in it. In order for them to leave you, they have to justify to themselves why they have put so much time and energy into their relationship with you. This forces them to come up with reasons for staying loyal to you, even when more favorable conditions might be found elsewhere.

When people don't have anything invested—emotionally, financially, or otherwise—they're quicker to jump ship. So get customers involved when things are going well—little by little, as part of a team or cause—and you will find they will stand by you in more difficult times.

Technique 4: The Power of Humility

President John F. Kennedy's approval rating went to a record high in 1961 after the Bay of Pigs fiasco, undoubtedly because it showed that he was human, fallible, and humbled. He made a mistake and took full responsibility for it.

If you are too full of yourself, there will be no room anyone else. No one wants to listen to, or follow, anyone who is egotistical. While you may get people to pay attention to you when they have to and when it suits them, when the going gets rough, they'll get going. They cannot be close to someone who is full of himself, as there is no room for anyone else.

Six Powerful Ways to Demonstrate Humility

1. Doing a job that some others might consider beneath them shows the world that you are a person *of* the people and that you are willing to do what it takes, at the expense of personal sacrifice, for the larger cause. The CEO who picks up trash from the factory floor inspires workers to do the same—and more.

2. The fastest way to lose someone's loyalty is to lie to him or her. Deceit equals arrogance, which is the opposite of humility. Even if the person does not like the news, your truthfulness speaks volumes and communicates an important message: *you can be trusted*. Moreover, people will take their chances with someone who is trustworthy over someone who tells them what they want to hear or who tries to cover up something. Always be honest and truthful in your dealings. This does not mean be blunt and rude. Rather, seek to be as kind and as respectful as you can, but never sacrifice the truth. Honesty illuminates fine character like a beacon in a fog of phonies.

3. Do not be a know-it-all, and when you are wrong, admit it. When you admit you are wrong, others realize that they are not going to be a bunch of lemmings following you off a cliff. Owning up to your errors shows responsibility as well as humility, two key traits that inspire loyalty.

4. When you do not know the answer to something, do not give one. Simply say, "I do not know." You'll be amazed at how much attention gets paid when you *do* have the answer to a question.

5. Treat everyone with respect, especially those from whom you don't need anything and who can't do anything for you. When you *have to* treat someone with great respect, you show their greatness. When you do the same for someone when you *don't* have to, it shows *your* greatness.

6. Share the credit. Whenever you are acknowledged for your work, be sure to mention each and every person who contributed, even in a small way, to your success.

If you do these few things, you will exemplify what it means to be humble. You will not be seen as weak, but as someone who is strong, and this strength will inspire others to attach themselves to you.

Strategy Review

- Bring people in on the inside and give them a little bit of power. They will have a harder time turning on you because you make them feel so special and important.
- We all want to attach ourselves to people of character. If you take a position that is unfavorable simply because it is right to do so, then long after the situation is forgotten, *you* will be remembered as a person of morality.

- Human beings have a strong need to act consistently. By slowly getting them involved with your causes, you help create a psychological commitment whereby they continue to support that which they have already supported.
- If you are too full of yourself, there will be no room for anyone else. You can show humility in simple ways such as being honest, admitting when you are wrong, not speaking when you do not know the answer, treating everyone with the proper respect, and sharing the credit for your accomplishments.

See These Chapters for Additional Strategies:

⇨ Chapter 3: **Make Anyone More Moral and Ethical**
⇨ Chapter 9: **Give the Gift of Self-Esteem**
⇨ Chapter 23: **Make Anyone More Respectful**

Chapter 5

Eliminate Prejudice in Anyone

Do you know people who are downright bigots or racists? The techniques presented in this chapter show you how to open their minds and get them to rethink their false and damaging beliefs. Of course it is naive to assume that you can eliminate their prejudices overnight. However, research has shown these approaches to be the most effective, and they will allow you to make inroads, if not great strides.

Technique 1: The Power of Emotions

Emotion creates motion. Emotions, not statistics, data, or cold hard facts, are the energy that fuels our thinking and choices in life. In fact, an estimated ninety percent of decisions are emotionally derived, and we then use logic to justify them.

Every time chain-smokers take a cigarette from the pack, they read that cigarette smoke may cause cancer. What are they thinking? *I could get hit by a bus tomorrow*, or *My aunt Sally lived to be one hundred years old, and she smoked every day since she was nine years of age?*

Reach a person's emotions, and you get to the real decision-maker within. There is nothing like startling images, or seeing something for yourself up close, to invoke emotions. In our morning newspaper we can read that two thousand people were killed in an earthquake in Chile, and then immediately glance at the gossip page, with barely an audible "How awful." But just one picture of a small girl sitting and crying in the rubble next to her mother who died in the earthquake does something more. It pulls at our heartstrings. It causes pain.

It has been said that anyone who visits a hot dog factory will never eat a hot dog again. Apparently the manufacturing process is so visually appalling that it is tough to get the images out of your head. Even though we may know that the U.S. Department of Agriculture permits a certain amount of hair, blood, and bone in hot dogs, seeing it for yourself is a whole other story.

EXAMPLE: *Your friend Erica thinks all immigrants are a drain on the economy and cannot turn out to be successful, contributing citizens.*

You might introduce Erica to someone who emigrated to the United States and became a success story. As she gets to know this individual as a person, not as someone who belongs to a group she dislikes, Erica will begin to rethink and then eventually readjust her attitude. Of course, one such encounter will not make Erica give up her prejudices, but it will begin the process of tearing them down.

Technique 2: A Firsthand Account

Technique 2 uses two powerful psychological processes: *social proof* and *cognitive dissonance*. Briefly, social proof is a power tool of influence that says when we see others, particularly those whom we respect and admire, do something, we are driven to adopt similar attitudes and behavior. This is why advertisers use celebrities in ads. The thinking is, *If this person whom I like uses this product, then I should too.*

Cognitive dissonance can be illustrated by the story that follows. Bill buys a watch for $500. Later, flipping through a magazine, he sees what seems to be the same watch advertised for $300. This produces an emotional inconsistency in Bill. He wants to see himself as a smart guy and a savvy shopper, yet the ad suggests evidence to the contrary. Bill can believe one of two scenarios: either he was duped and he overpaid, or the advertisement is not what it appears to be. His level of self-esteem determines the outcome. If he has high self-esteem, he will believe he made a mistake. If he has low self-esteem, he will believe he was cheated. Either way, something has to give in order to reconcile the balance sheet of Bill's life and reduce the cognitive dissonance — the emotional pain caused by this conflict.

Technique 2 intertwines social proof and cognitive dissonance, as illustrated in the following.

EXAMPLE: *Your son thinks people of a certain race or religion are bad.*

Have someone your son respects explain why his attitude is wrong. Not only do you gain the power of social proof, but this also engages cognitive dissonance, as your son has to reconcile his affection for this person with his own prejudices. Can someone he respects so much be wrong about this? Something has to give.

Now, as we saw in the "Bill" example, the higher a person's self-esteem, the more likely he is to let go of his prejudice. Simply, if he's feeling good about himself, *he* can be wrong. Mood is the shadow of self-esteem. When we're in a good mood, we temporarily feel better about ourselves and our life.

Before you apply Technique 2, put your son in a better mood, and he will have the emotional fuel to let go of his damaging belief. A quick way to do this is to get him excited about something. For example, suggest that the two of you go to a play, to dinner, to the movies. Or maybe promise him a sleepover with some friends or a camping trip he's been talking about.

Technique 3: Acts of Kindness

If one person in particular is the object of a person's scorn then, if possible, have this individual do an act of kindness for this prejudiced person. It will be difficult for him to dislike someone who is kind to him despite his biased feelings. Faced with this conflict, he will have to adjust his thinking to accommodate the possibility that he may have misjudged this person.

EXAMPLE: *Mr. Jones thinks Peter's lifestyle as a "swinging bachelor" is objectionable.*

Peter doesn't have to do anything grand or magnificent, just a small gesture such as shoveling the snow from Jones's driveway so he can get his car out, or going out of his way to pick something up for him. It's important for Peter not to wait around for a pat on the back. Not "owning up" to the kind deed displays more about his character. That he did it because it was right, and not to be liked. This is a further dent in the thinking of the prejudiced person.

WHY, OH WHY?

Keep asking why. When a person holds a certain belief, ask why. And when he answers those questions, ask why again. For instance, a young girl makes fun of people who are different. You ask her why, and she says, "Everyone does it." So you ask why again. She says it makes her popular. You again ask why. By repeatedly asking why, you get to the core of why she does what she does, and so you get her to think about it herself. As a result, she is forced to come face-to-face with her unkind behavior.

Technique 4: Houston, We Have Contact

Landmark research by Gordon Allport (1954) on the nature of prejudice concludes that contact between two groups of equal status, in pursuit of common goals, can decrease prejudices. Therefore, try to get a prejudiced person to be part of an activity—for example, a sport, business pursuit, community project—with the very people toward whom he holds a prejudice. Be sure, though, that you commingle the different people and that you do not pit one group against the other.

Other studies suggest that when a member of a group relies on the others in order to complete a task, liking of group members increased. Therefore, cooperation within the group is a necessary component in order to achieve success.

EXAMPLE: *A camp counselor wants to reduce tensions between boys of different backgrounds.*

The counselor has the boys compete in various competitions—anything from building a tree house to a three-legged race. As the individuals begin to work within a group against a common "enemy," they develop a sense of camaraderie and they question even long-held prejudices.

Strategy Review

- Emotions fuel our thinking and choices. Turn those cold facts into real people with real stories.
- Engage the laws of social proof and cognitive dissonance by having someone a biased individual respects explain why he does not hold the same prejudiced belief.
- If it's personal, then perform an act of kindness for the prejudiced person. This forces him to reexamine his thinking.
- Studies show that when people of different groups, with a similar social status, work together toward a common goal, their prejudices are reduced.

See This Chapter for Additional Strategies:
⇨ Chapter 23: **Make Anyone More Respectful**

Chapter 6

Change the Parent Who Doesn't Spend Enough Time with the Kids

While we would like to believe that parents make spending time with their children a priority, this is not always the case. Instead, many mothers and fathers today find they do not have enough time for their offspring because they are overburdened by the many responsibilities of life. The following techniques offer you a variety of strategies to get such parents to find more time for their children.

Technique 1: The Neighbors Are Watching

Sometimes a little social pressure may be needed, for example, to get a father more motivated. To accomplish this, the mother sets up father-and-son or father-and-daughter activities in the neighborhood. Now the dad will be shamed into going because his wife is the one who created the event. And she will be getting not just one family to spend more time together, but a whole neighborhood.

EXAMPLE: *A wife wants her husband to spend more time with their kids.*

The wife arranges for father-and-child activities—such as softball games, model-car racing, and sculpting contests—to be held in the neighborhood once a week or a few times a month. Not only will the children spend time with the father *during* the activity, but also during all of the preparing and planning that goes into it.

Technique 2: Make a Trade

Time is in short supply these days. It is one thing to want parents to spend more time with their children; it's another to help them do it. Make it as easy as possible for them to be able to take the time. In this way, even if, sadly, the parents do not have an overwhelming desire to spend time with the kids, they will not feel as if they are "wasting" their time and should be doing something else; you are trading what they *have* to do for what you *want* them to do.

EXAMPLE: *A grandmother wants her son and daughter-in-law to spend more time with their children.*

The parents complain that they are simply too busy. So one Sunday, instead of the parents being busy with the usual chores—mowing the lawn, doing laundry, food shopping—the grandmother agrees to take over these responsibilities for the day. Now the parents are free to do things with their children without feeling guilty about "wasting" time or worrying about chores and other responsibilities.

Technique 3: Mutual Satisfaction

Parents who do not see the necessity of spending more time with their children will be more inclined to do so if it is enjoyable. So come up with hobbies, sports, and the like that both parents and child enjoy. Then they can spend time together and build a relationship in a way that offers the parents an opportunity to do what they love anyway.

EXAMPLE: *You want your son from a previous marriage and your husband to spend more time together.*

Find an activity that they both enjoy doing. Whether it's karate, model airplanes, fishing, art, or cooking doesn't matter. Common interests often create mutual affection and trust, so when two people are engaged in an activity they both enjoy, it creates a stronger bond between them.

A GOOD INVESTMENT

A father is crucial to a child's emotional and intellectual growth. Research shows that a father's involvement has a great impact on both a child's behavior and learning skills. In fact, children whose fathers actively participate in their lives have higher math and reading scores than do other children.

Technique 4: Be Practical

A mother who is well-meaning finds the day simply gets away from her. Thus she needs to take practical steps to insure that the day does not end without her doing what needs to be done—in this case, spending quality time with her children. Note that the *amount* of time is less significant than the *quality*. For example, watching TV with a child does *not* constitute spending time together, and it offers zero emotional satisfaction to the child.

EXAMPLE: *Jim wants his wife, Marie, who works two jobs, to have more time for their daughter.*

Of course if Marie can give up one of her jobs, all the better. But if this is not possible, then Jim and Marie need to arrange a set time for her to be with their little girl. For example, Marie could set aside one hour a night and a half-day Sunday when she and her daughter spend time together without interruption. Instead of trying to work the child into her day, Marie works the day around her child. This time is set in stone, and no matter what comes up, they try to work around it. This arrangement conveys to the little girl that she is a priority, and all children need this to feel that they are truly loved and valued.

Technique 5: The Power of Hypocrisy

Studies show that human behavior is most readily changed when two things happen: (1) when we agree that we *should* be doing something and (2) when inconsistencies are pointed out between our attitude and our behavior. For example, a study was conducted in California on a college campus in a women's locker room. Women entering to shower were asked to sign a petition that read: *Take shorter showers. Turn shower off while soaping up. If I can do it, so can you.* And then the researchers added one thing. They asked the women to answer questions about their showering habits, including the question, When showering, do you always turn off the water while soaping up or shampooing?

The women who signed the form urging others to conserve water *and* who were made aware of their apparent hypocrisy then took showers that were half as long as those who either signed the petition or answered questions about their showering habits but did not do both. The one-two punch is extremely effective. When people express an attitude and then are reminded of their previous failures to live up to it, a powerful motivational force is created (Dickerson et al. 1992).

EXAMPLE: *Kelly wants her husband, Sam, who travels often for business, to spend more time with their children.*

Kelly asks Sam to sign a petition or to write a small article for a newsletter about the importance of the father's role in a child's life. Since it doesn't cost him anything, he's likely to oblige. Then after a short while Kelly asks him when was the last time he spent quality time with their kids.

The power of the psychology in play is amazing. Unconsciously Sam is driven to correct the hypocrisy, and so becomes more motivated to be with his children. Now if Kelly were to suggest he take the kids camping, he is far more likely to agree. And she does not need to remind him that he signed the petition. As long as he was aware of what he was signing, he won't soon forget, specifically because it was incongruous with his behavior.

Strategy Review

- Use the power of social pressure to get parents to spend more time with their children, even though they may not be that interested in doing so on their own.
- If parents do not have enough time to spend time with their children, then trade what they have to do for what

you want them to do. They will agree because they will not feel they are losing out on doing something more important.

- The best way to get a parent and child to spend more time together is to find something that they both have an interest in. This way, even if they do not enjoy being with each other, they will enjoy the time spent. And, you greatly increase the possibility of them eventually enjoying each other's company.

- Instead of trying to find time for parents to spend with their children, arrange a time and then work their schedule around it. Not only does this ensure that Mom and Dad will have time with their offspring, but it communicates to the children that they are a priority, not an afterthought.

- Engage the power of psychology by bringing out inconsistencies between parents' values and their actual behavior. Something has to give, and so their thinking will be transformed.

See These Chapters for Additional Strategies:

⇨ Chapter   3: **Make Anyone More Moral and Ethical**
⇨ Chapter   9: **Give the Gift of Self-Esteem**
⇨ Chapter 26: **Make Anyone More Interested in Anything**

Chapter 7

Motivate Anyone to Lose Weight

Almost all of us want to be healthy and to look our best, but we often lose out to an inner struggle. Therefore getting someone to lose weight is not a matter of convincing the person to do so, but rather of making it *easier* emotionally for him or her to do so. The five psychological techniques presented in this chapter help you to clear an emotional path to change a person's eating habits and attitudes toward health.

Technique 1: Please Help Me

You can help someone lose weight by having him do things for *you*. If you ask him not to buy sweets because you don't want them in the house, or to join a gym with you so that it makes it easier for you to work out, you get him to change his habits without consciously agreeing to do so. Additionally, often a person will do something for someone else more readily than he would for himself. So he's happy to oblige, and once he begins to lose weight, you build momentum and increase his desire to get—and stay—in better shape.

EXAMPLE: *Your husband needs to lose weight but doesn't know it.*

If your husband needs to drop a few pounds, you might say something like, "Dear, I want to try to get into shape for the summer, but you know I have no willpower. If we can keep candy and cake out of the house, it will be a big help to me. And I find working out so boring, why don't we walk together around the lake? Or maybe you can join the gym with me. Also, I want to try some new low-fat, low-carbohydrate recipes that a friend told me about; I'll pick up the ingredients, and we'll cook it tonight."

This technique can be effective because you want your husband to be in good shape, he wants to help you to achieve your goals, and all the while you are achieving your aim of getting him into shape.

AN AFFAIR TO REMEMBER

The ego can work for or against us. While a person may not have the willpower to lose weight for health reasons, vanity is another story. Thus a person with a clear-cut objective and deadline will often be inspired to shed excess pounds. So come up with a reason to celebrate— a wedding, reunion, anniversary—and you'll help create a powerful motivating force for someone to lose weight.

Technique 2: Strike While the Iron Is Hot

Anything that is put off until Monday will probably be put off again. Inspiration comes with a built-in window of opportunity, so whenever people are motivated to change, help them to do so. By not delaying action, you engage cognitive dissonance—that is, the unconscious mind adopts the belief that what they are doing is important to *them.* If you take immediate action, something actually becomes more important.

EXAMPLE: *Tom wants his wife, Patricia, to be more interested in a healthier lifestyle.*

Whenever Patricia mentions anything related to being healthier, Tom moves mountains to help her accomplish it. For example, if she says it might be fun to go hiking, he goes online and books a hiking trip. Should Patricia want to cook more nutritious meals, Tom goes with her to buy some new cookbooks. Catch the wave of inspiration when you can, and you will be surprised how long you can ride it.

Keep in mind the act of building psychological momentum, so even if you don't think it's worth the effort for one time, you create movement and begin to reshape the person's behavior on a more permanent level.

Technique 3: Part of a Pattern

Behavioral change is easiest to make when the new behavior is incorporated within the context of a routine or pattern. So avoid isolating the behavior. For instance, if you want your son to do his homework, sandwich in the new behavior between things he really likes. When he comes home from school, he first has a snack, then does his homework, and then plays outside. The order should always be the same, and the time should be as consistent as possible.

EXAMPLE: *Together, a couple wants to lose weight and exercise more.*

The couple should set up a fixed time and place to work out. In addition, what they do before and afterward should always be the same. So after work, four days a week, they go to the gym together, following a set routine. Afterward they come home for dinner with the family, and then play a game with the kids. By making exercise part of their schedule and not an addition to it, the couple is more likely to stick with it.

Technique 4: The Power of Kindness

To make it easy for a person to lose weight, offer the necessary psychological nourishment. The psychology is similar to that used when helping someone who is engaging in self-destructive behavior. We will summarize two key elements here, but for more in-depth information, see Chapter 10.

- Many people constantly criticize the person they are trying to help. However, it is far more effective to give only positive reinforcement for positive behavior and to say nothing when the person falls short.
- An essential ingredient of healing is unconditional love or, when more appropriate, simple acceptance. The person must know that you love him and/or respect him for who he is, unconditionally. According to an old expression, "That which goes out of the heart goes into the heart." If you truly have his best interest at heart, he will perceive it as such.

EXAMPLE: *Chuck wants to help his wife lose weight and get into shape.*

Chuck uses the aforementioned two ideas, saying to his wife, "Sweetheart, I want you to know that I think you are doing great. I know it's not easy for you, and I am very proud of your progress. But I also want you to know that if you decide that you are going back to the old ways, that's fine too. I love you. I will love you no matter what you do. I think it's great that you are losing weight, and for as long as you do, you have my full and unconditional support." Chuck says this often. In fact, he cannot say it enough times.

Technique 5: Connect on a Deeper Level

A man was very obese, and although he tried everything possible to lose weight, he just could not keep the pounds off. Then his daughter needed a kidney transplant, and while he could donate a kidney of his own, the doctors could not perform the operation because of his weight. He then proceeded to lose 160 pounds in order to give his kidney to his child.

If a father, for instance, were to think what it would be like if he had a heart attack and died, leaving a young son without a father and causing injurious effects that will forever discolor the boy's life, he might rethink his eating habits. Being reminded of the suffering he would cause his parents, siblings, or friends will also make him think twice about how he lives his life. While he may not be motivated himself, illuminating the suffering he would cause others by not taking better care of himself can be a powerful motivator.

EXAMPLE: *Emily, a single mother, wants to help her father lose weight.*

Emily might say, "You know, Dad, the kids will miss you terribly if anything happens to you. You know how attached they are to you. You're the only father figure in their life. They look up to you, and they need you. If you don't want to exercise and eat better for yourself, maybe you would do it for them." Emily's words make it harder for her father to overindulge, because now he has a reason to feel guilty. As a result, she may find he has an increased desire to lose weight.

Strategy Review

- Don't make being fit about the other person, but about you. In this way the person will help you to lose weight, while you accomplish your goal of helping the person to get into shape.
- Ride the wave of inspiration. Whenever people express an interest in doing what you want them to, take action right away to build momentum.
- Behavioral change is easiest to make when the new behavior is incorporated within the context of a routine or pattern.
- Increase the ease with which you get someone to adopt a new behavior by giving positive reinforcement and offering unconditional love and respect.
- Help people to realize the importance of taking care of themselves by having them consider that others would suffer if they were to suffer from poor health, or worse.

See These Chapters for Additional Strategies:

⇨ Chapter   9: **Give the Gift of Self-Esteem**
⇨ Chapter 23: **Make Anyone More Respectful**
⇨ Chapter 26: **Make Anyone More Interested in Anything**

How to Change Anyone's Emotional State

Turn the Unhappy into the Happy and the Neurotic into the Normal, and Make Anyone Feel Emotionally Stable, Happier, and Balanced. Whether it is your Patient, Parent, Friend, or Spouse, Permanently Shift Anyone's State for the Better.

Silence is the best medicine for your welfare.

—AVOS 1:17

Chapter 8

A Quick-Fix Pick-Me-Up:
Turn Anyone's Mood
Around, Fast

Do you have people in your life who are perpetual sad sacks, a drain on everyone around them? Give them a quick shot of emotional adrenaline by using any of the psychological strategies that follow, and snap them into a better mood. Try these techniques on yourself too, if you want to go from pessimist to optimist lightning fast.

Technique 1: A Long-Term Investment

To think and behave in a way that says, "I care about me," is essential for our well-being. When we live only for today, we send a message to our unconscious that says, "I do not care what happens to me tomorrow." This harms us emotionally.

Have you ever joined a gym and then found yourself to be in an unusually good mood? You didn't lift a single weight or swim a single lap. Why did you feel so good? Because you sent a message to your unconscious that said, "I am making an investment in me." When we ignore ourselves, it is just as if someone else were to ignore us; we cannot help but feel lousy. By encouraging someone to take a specific action that says, "I like me enough to put time and energy into who I am," you help him to reestablish a sense of self-worth, and that puts him into a better mood.

EXAMPLE: *You want to snap your sister-in-law Maggie out of her blues.*

Encourage Maggie to set objective(s) that have long-term benefits—for example, making a dentist appointment, cleaning out the attic, establishing a retirement fund. Actions like these will makes Maggie feel better because she is taking responsibility for, and investing in, herself. (It doesn't matter whether the actions themselves, such as going to the dentist, are intrinsically unpleasant.) Ideally, you should encourage Maggie periodically to set long-term goals. Eventually, she will begin to focus on the future, not on immediate satisfaction.

Technique 2: Pure Joy

Well-meaning people often try to get a depressed person to do enjoyable things, but they soon find that an unhappy person is an unwilling partner.

Depressed people need to feel alive. Joy, the anticipation of something pleasurable, is different from happiness. People who are in a poor mood may have difficulty enjoying themselves. Their mind races, their thoughts are chaotic, and they are simply tired, emotionally drained. They feel like the world is "out there," and they cannot extract pleasure from it; they cannot connect.

However, if they're given something to look forward to, depressed people can plan, and they can lose themselves in their thoughts about this wonderful future event. This not only gives them something positive to be consumed with, it also makes it easier for them to make changes in their life. When we are excited about something, we come out of our shell, connect more to life, and thus want to be more a part of the world.

Even those who "have it together" can find themselves a little blue after the holidays. These blues result because no matter how great the holidays were, they could never have lived up to the ideal. When everything is over, people can feel sad because the buildup was so great, and the reality could not compete with the anticipation.

EXAMPLE: *Your wife has been moping around the house for days.*

Find something your wife will be excited about, and arrange it for a few weeks down the road. It can be anything from a vacation to cosmetic surgery to a visit from out-of-town friends. This emotional carrot will keep her focused on positive and happy thoughts. If necessary, cycle through a revolving array of carrots until she is able to generate enough internal pleasure from doing, and then eventually from simply being.

I MUST HAVE THAT!

Late-night infomercials exploit this quirk of human nature more than any other. Do you know that studies have shown that over 80 percent of the people who order a self-improvement product from television never even open the box it comes in? What motivates these night owls? By picking up the phone and ordering the latest miracle product (showing them how to make money, become a real estate baron, or go from fat to thin in a week), they're filled with the joy of anticipation.

Technique 3: Time Is Life

Living contradictory to our values drains us. A reasonable father would not sell his son for ten million dollars. But this same dad may spend very little time with that boy. This forces him to justify his actions in a myriad of ways, but in the end this rationalizing is draining. It too creates a division within him—an emotional battle. He cannot simultaneously believe that X is all-important and spend his time, energy, and effort on Y. In order to remain emotionally solvent, he must live, at least to some extent, in accordance with his values and what he really wants in life.

EXAMPLE: *As a therapist, you have a patient, Arthur, who cannot seem to get out of his funk.*

Prioritizing helps to simplify, harmonize, and synchronize our thoughts and life. Encourage Arthur to be authentic and genuine in one area of life and then, in some small way, to move in that direction. If he's always wanted to be a painter, have him buy paints and canvases; if he believes relationships are important, have him forgive, or apologize to, someone with whom he no longer speaks. People cannot completely ignore what they believe is important. Moving towards something personally meaningful will help jolt Arthur out of his blues, as well as add to his emotional strength and courage.

LET THE GAMES BEGIN

People who are in a lousy mood are filled with both emotional and physical negativity. They are in a *constricted consciousness*, where they cannot see outside their own wants and needs. Get them to participate in a physical game, a dance, aerobics, or a sport so they can get their body moving. Such activity also releases endorphins, changing their physiology and helping to put them in better spirits.

Technique 4: Enough about You

A divorced woman is unhappy. Get her to do something *for you* by asking for her help or advice. Turning her focus from herself to another is a terrific way to elevate her mood. Psychologically, it works because you make her feel good about herself in three distinct ways. First, you demonstrate trust, making her feel trustworthy, and so better about who she is. Next, you give her the chance to contribute, which helps her feel more self-reliant. Giving to others makes us feel independent and important, and we need this sense of freedom to feel good about ourselves. Finally, you take her focus off her own problems. The less time she spends consumed with herself, the less energy she gives to negativity.

EXAMPLE: *You want to help Carolyn, a recently divorced coworker, to feel better about things.*

- Ask for her advice and input, and encourage her to offer suggestions to any challenges that you may be facing. You might say, "Carolyn, you're so good with people; can you help me come up with a game plan for dealing with the contractor?" or "You know computers better than anyone; what's the best way to configure my hard drive for maximum speed?"

If you can take Carolyn's advice and then follow up with a call or a card of appreciation, all the better. Carolyn can give you her time, advice, and thoughts—it doesn't matter. As long as she is moving in the direction of giving and not taking, her mood will lift.

- Ask Carolyn to help you with a project, and allow her to be in charge of herself as much as you can. Depending upon the situation, at the very least ask her to do something, and give her full autonomy in the planning and execution. For instance, you might ask her to supervise a training program, hire and train a new receptionist, or redecorate the lobby.

Strategy Review

- It is essential for our emotional well-being to think and behave in a way that says, "I care about me." Encourage objective(s) that have a long-term benefit.
- Living contradictory to our values drains us. Help others to be authentic, to be genuine in what they want out of life, and to move in some small way in that direction.
- Find an event that a depressed person will be excited about, and schedule it for a few weeks down the road. This emotional carrot will keep the person focused on positive, happy thoughts and will make changes easier.
- Give depressed individuals a chance to contribute. By taking the focus off themselves and demonstrating faith and trust in their abilities, you help to instill them with a temporary sense of confidence and emotional well-being.

See these chapters for Additional Strategies:

⇨ Chapter 9: **Give the Gift of Self-Esteem**
⇨ Chapter 15: **Turn a Lazy Bum into an Ambitious Go-Getter**
⇨ Chapter 23: **Make Anyone More Respectful**

Give the Gift of Self-Esteem: Help Anyone Like Himself More

Self-respect is the gateway to self-esteem. Simply, we like ourselves when we respect ourselves. But how do we gain self-respect? We gain it when we do what is right over what is easy—or over that which only makes us look good. When we don't act this way, we literally like ourselves less.

Within all of us, three inner forces are at odds with each other: the body, the ego (or lower soul), and the (higher) soul. The body wants to escape from life through sleep, entertainment, and endless distraction; the ego craves attention and control; and the soul wants to do what is right.

Doing what is easy or comfortable is a *body drive*. Overindulgences of this nature include overeating or oversleeping, in effect doing or not doing something because of how it feels. An *ego drive* can run the gamut from making a joke at someone else's expense to buying a car we cannot afford. In essence, we do something so that we appear in a certain way to others. When we are driven by ego, we do things that project the "right" image, and we become consumed with power and prestige, things that many people value as ends in themselves, and not as a means to something more meaningful. Our choices are then not based on what is good, but rather on what makes us look good. When we do this, we are not in control of ourselves.

However, when we make a choice to do what is right, we feel good about ourselves. Only when we are able to choose responsibly—and do so—do we gain self-respect and, in return, self-esteem. This is how self-respect and self-control are intertwined. People who are not in "control" of themselves and what they really want have no self-respect, as they are slaves either to society or to their own impulses.

This explains *control freaks*. When they do not get the respect they hunger for, the ego's ultimate weapon, *anger*, engages. It is a defense mechanism against feelings of vulnerability. Anger is the illusion of control that makes them feel powerful, when in fact they are out of control. And the less control people have over themselves, the more they try to control the lives of others. They need to be in charge of something, and since they cannot get traction in their own lives, they seek to do it through influencing the lives of others. These people are often well-meaning. They do want to help. They just come off a bit insistent and pushy because their ego needs for them to be effective. And that can only happen if you take their advice.

DOES HE LIKE HIMSELF?

A quick way to tell if a person has self-esteem is to observe how he treats himself *and* others. A person who lacks self-esteem may indulge in things for himself to satisfy only his own desires, and he will not treat others particularly well. Or he may overly cater to others because he craves their approval and respect, but not take care of his own needs. Only someone who truly has self-respect will treat both himself and others well. And when we say "well," we do not mean he engages in short-term gratification. Rather, he invests in his long-term well-being as well by being kind and good to others, not so they will like him, but because he likes them or because it is the right thing to do.

People who have control over themselves have the freedom to choose, and this sense of independence sets off an emotional chain reaction. This chain includes a variety of "ingredients" that, when present, balance the psyche, and when missing, throw people off. The solution is to infuse people who lack self-esteem with these components to restore them to an emotionally healthy place, rich with self-esteem.

Seven Keys to Installing Self-Esteem

KEY 1: HUMAN BEINGS NEED TO BE MOVING

Did you know that successful health clubs usually have hundreds of new members join every month? Yet the clubs never add one new locker. How can you have hundreds of people joining a club without the owners screaming, "Get the hammer ready, and knock down the wall; we need two hundred more lockers immediately"? The answer is that health clubs understand human nature. People become elated when they decide to join. They love going to the club, sitting down with the membership person, and signing up. They'll spend hundreds of dollars and lots of hours shopping for a gym bag, sneakers, headbands, warm-up clothes. They're all excited, and they haven't even broken into a sweat yet. Why? Because they are moving forward.

If you are not moving toward a meaningful objective, then you cannot be fulfilled. There is no status quo in nature. In order to feel good, to feel alive, human beings need to be striving, moving forward. We are hardwired, driven, to move.

As the health-club illustration shows, having an objective is one thing, but in order to insure continual movement, key aspects that nourish the psyche and soul must be implemented as well. Let's clarify this idea.

EXAMPLE: *You want your daughter to feel better about herself.*

The dynamics of the relationship will best determine the type of objective or job you give your daughter. How big it is doesn't matter, as long it is significant to her. The only criterion is that it be something she will enjoy doing. For instance, for a child it could be a hobby or sport; for a patient you could have him start a small non-profit company.

KEY 2: THE EGO NEEDS MEASURABLE TRACTION

Full-sized circus elephants are kept with a small rope looped around one leg. They don't try to break free because when they were young and weaker, they were tethered the same way, and after trying and trying to escape, at some point they gave up. As adults they could easily tear down the whole circus tent and move about, but they have learned helplessness and so they don't even try.

Learned helplessness, a term coined by psychologist Martin Seligman, exists when a person feels that since she is not in control she might as well give up. Seligman contended that people are helpless when their actions are perceived as not influencing their outcomes.

People need to believe that if they do action X, it will produce result Y. When people do not believe that they can change anything in their life, they lose traction and the will to do *anything*.

Such people need to be reminded that their actions produce results. If they believe that their actions are futile, then they will understandably conclude that they have no control. That is enough to make anyone depressed and frustrated.

It can drive people crazy to feel that it doesn't matter what they do; it makes no difference and causes no effect. And since it is easier to damage than it is to create, emotionally unwell people often go for the quick emotional fix: they will make a destructive impact just for effect or to gain attention, rather than labor in positive, constructive pursuits.

For true emotional well-being, however, people must feel that they are making a positive measurable difference. A drop in the ocean does not inspire us, but results lead to the desire for more growth and movement. It may not be enough for people to get the feeling that things are happening; in their darker hours their ego may need to point to indisputable, concrete proof that they are doing something real.

Devise a way for measuring an individual's success so that he can evaluate the effectiveness of his progress. He should feel that he is effective, that he has traction and can exert influence over something, or change it. A person who lacks self-esteem may feel as though he is floating, with no anchor. This component will help him to feel more grounded and stable.

Everything in nature has a cycle, and so if he can actually finish something that he started, not only does he gain a sense of accomplishment but he also feels more fulfilled from having successfully seen something through to the end. So ideally, progress should come in the form of completing segments of his objective so his minisuccesses are self-contained and continue to lift his self-esteem.

EXAMPLE: *Your employee Irma lacks the confidence she needs to perform better.*

Give Irma an objective—for instance, organizing the company's annual dinner. Then work together—or have her do it herself—to list the specific tasks that need to be done. This to-do list includes everything from finding a meeting place to sending out invitations. Then once a week review her progress. As Irma begins to check off things on her list, she will feel the pride of progress.

KEY 3: A SENSE OF INDEPENDENCE AND AUTONOMY

Freedom is being able to choose to do what you want to do. As we said, a person can only choose when he is in control of himself. And this person, who lacks self-esteem, does not. Whenever we exercise true free will in a meaningful direction, we gain pleasure because it moves us to emotional freedom and stability. This person is having difficulty exercising her free will, so in order to ignite that aspect of her psyche, *we give her this sense of freedom.*

Therefore the objective, pursuit, or job that she engages in should have an element of autonomy. She should have the ability to make decisions and then bear the consequences; these are the very same dynamics that should exist within her everyday life but do not.

Ideally you would want to have her work toward it, but it is unlikely you will be afforded the luxury of dealing with someone who is willing to invest in herself without an immediate payoff. So initially, while she can be given the gift of this objective, she must rise or fall by her own efforts. When we invest in anything, including ourselves, we appreciate "us" more. In trying to reestablish cause and effect, a person has to feel that she is responsible for the results. She has to realize that while the opportunity itself may be a gift of sorts, it is only through her effort that she made it successful.

EXAMPLE: *Your teenage son Henry is socially awkward and lacks self-esteem.*

Give Henry a task with measurable rungs, and then back off. Don't be a nervous Nellie, and avoid the temptation to ask him how thing are going (outside of the progress review). It will do little good to put Henry in a key role only to micromanage everything he does. He must be given free rein to do whatever is feasible and practical. Therefore, if you put him in charge of balancing the family budget so that you can all take a vacation, don't scrutinize every bill and every choice he makes. When he wants to talk about it, listen encouragingly and attentively. Otherwise let your silence demonstrate your confidence in his ability.

KEY 4: MEANING AND A SENSE OF PERMANENCE

Whenever we do something that has meaning, it gives meaning to our lives. And meaning is pleasurable. Everything in creation serves a purpose beyond itself. Every cell in the human body and every drop of water in the ocean is in a symbiotic relationship with the larger organism; it is an integral part of a larger purpose, serving an even greater function. It goes beyond itself, transcends itself.

The accompanying diagram presents psychologist Abraham Maslow's Hierarchy of Needs. Starting at the bottom, it shows the most basic needs necessary for survival; as each is met, we strive higher to greater emotional fulfillment.

Self-
Actualization
Pursue Inner Talent
Creativity Fulfillment

Self-Esteem
Achievement Mastery
Recognition Respect

Belonging-Love
Friends Family Spouse Lover

Safety
Security Stability Freedom from Fear

Physiological
Food Water Shelter Warmth

HIERARCHY OF NEEDS

In order to feel completely fulfilled, we need to be a part of something that connects to a larger whole. We all operate under the canopy of human nature—it is inescapable, unchangeable, and universal.

In order to obtain the highest level of fulfillment, or *self-actualization*, we need to have a positive impact on someone, something other than ourselves. In order to feel good about ourselves, we must feel good about what we are doing.

EXAMPLE: *You are working with your friend Nyasia to help her feel better about herself.*

In order to engage self-actualization, attach an altruistic component to Nyasia's objective. Regardless of what it is, it has to benefit someone besides herself. Let her know clearly what she is doing is helping others.

KEY 5: THE CREATIVE COMPONENT

Nothing in nature is identical to anything else in nature. Indeed, even identical twins have different fingerprints. We human beings derive such intense satisfaction from creative thought and action, the feeling we get is unparalleled. It locks in our attention and individuality.

Have you ever noticed how much pleasure a small child gets from drawing a picture? Or even coloring? We are driven to be unique, to express ourselves.

When we are creating, we feel alive. To simply do, to not be creative in any way, has the potential for shutting us down. Creativity allows us to tap into the source of inspiration and impart our own sense of individuality to the world.

EXAMPLE: *Phil wants to help his brother Tom to feel better about himself.*

When Phil gives Tom autonomy, he should allow him to be as creative as he wants. So if Phil puts his brother in charge of his art showing, Phil should let him be free to be original in the theme, location, activities, and so on. Such responsibility will add tremendously to Tom's self-esteem and emotional well-being. Otherwise it will not matter how successful Tom is, because he will not feel the pride of creative expression.

NOW, NOW, NOW

Although the current self-help arena talks about "being in the moment," there is no contradiction in the concept of moving forward. Being in the moment is not about stagnation; it is about enjoying who you are, where you are, and what you have. A person who is happy with his lot looks to expand and grow. It is the one who is depressed and miserable who wants to crawl into a hole and die. Only by moving forward and feeling good about himself can he come to appreciate what he has and be in the proverbial *now*.

KEY 6: GOOD, RIGHT, AND TRUE

You cannot do the right thing the wrong way. Lack of integrity saps our energy. It is like having one foot on the gas and one on the brake. An individual will burn out, dragged down by his conscience. Should he become aware that he does not feel good about what he is doing, he may be forced into justification, which is also very draining. When our thoughts conflict with our actions, we are in spiritual, emotional, and physical discord.

A person who seeks self-esteem needs to act in accordance with a solid moral barometer. Otherwise he is sacrificing long-term satisfaction for an immediate payoff. And this is precisely what he has been doing for too long. To stem the tide, you must have him pursue his objective with integrity so that in the long run he wins by doing what is right. Do not let him cut corners; intervene if he does. And encourage him to find win-win solutions to problems so that no one winds up getting a raw deal.

EXAMPLE: *Theresa wants to help her assistant, Susan, to have more self-esteem.*

During her weekly reviews, Theresa makes sure that progress doesn't come at the expense of honesty. For instance, if Susan is trying to get the best price for a keynote speaker, she should not lie about the number of attendees. Theresa should make sure that Susan is honest with her. Should Susan fall short in meeting agreed-upon expectations, Theresa should create a warm and understanding atmosphere, and work with Susan to get back on track so she will feel comfortable being open when she has problems with the project.

Strategy Review

To get someone to like who he is, he has to feel that he is someone who is capable of doing what is right and being effective in what he chooses to do. This gives him both self-respect and self-efficacy. Thus, self-esteem naturally emerges.

By having him work towards a meaningful objective that produces tangible results, you infuse his psyche with an unwavering sense of self-respect. This gives him energy and fuels his thirst for life, investing more in himself and even moving away from self-destructive behaviors. If we feel as though we are doing something significant, then we have traction in this world. We no longer feel neurotic, a plaything at the whim of circumstance. Instead, our desire to escape is replaced by a strong motivation to be part of the world.

This psychological strategy gives him what he did not have in his own world: independence, a feeling of accomplishment, and creative, positive expression. As his psyche is nourished with these vital ingredients, he will become more and more stable; his perspective will broaden, and his attitudes and behaviors will become more emotionally balanced. In short he becomes someone who simply likes himself. And you have given him the gift of self-esteem.

See These Chapters for Additional Strategies:
➪ Chapter   3: **Make Anyone More Moral and Ethical**
➪ Chapter   8: **A Quick-Fix Pick-Me-Up**
➪ Chapter 10: **Eliminate Anyone's Self-Destructive Behaviors**
➪ Chapter 23: **Make Anyone More Respectful**

Eliminate Anyone's Self-destructive Behaviors

From smoking to drinking to an unhealthy lifestyle, if you want to help someone kick bad habits and get his life back on track, then follow these step-by-step techniques. This discussion on the psychology in play picks up from the previous chapter.

When we give into our impulses and do what we feel like doing instead of what we know we should do, we feel lousy. And in an attempt to feel better we engage in more things to make us happy— now, at the expense of tomorrow. This cycle continues to spiral downward, because when we do not feel good about ourselves we seek the hollow, temporary refuge of immediate gratification. As a result, we succumb to our impulses even more instead of rising above them.

When endless entertainment and distractions no longer dull the pain, a person may turn to drugs and alcohol to escape. A self-destructive lifestyle is a bid to numb the mental anguish of seeing his life as it is; it is also an unconscious punishment for allowing himself to get to the position where he now finds himself.

INTERVENTION?

Intervention is a process of confronting a drug or alcohol abuser whereby the people who have been affected, harmed, or injured by his behavior—family, friends, and employers—tell him in their own words how his behavior has negatively affected their lives. The objective is to get the person into a treatment program. While some intervenors have met with success, others have found that intervention further alienates the abuser from what is left of his support system. If intervention works, great, but if it doesn't the situation may become even more difficult.

A Two-Hundred-Year-Old Story

A royal prince once went mad and thought he was a turkey. He felt compelled to sit naked under the table, pecking at bones and pieces of bread like a turkey. The royal physicians gave up all hope of curing him of this madness, and the king suffered tremendous grief.

A sage came and said, "I will undertake to cure him."

Then the sage undressed and sat naked under the table next to the prince, pecking at crumbs and bones.

"Who are you?" asked the prince. "What are you doing here?"

"And you?" replied the sage. "What are you doing here?"

"I am a turkey," said the prince.

"I am also a turkey," answered the sage.

They sat together like this for some time, and eventually they became good friends. One day the sage signaled the king's servants to throw him his shirt. He said to the prince, "What makes you think that a turkey can't wear a shirt? You can wear a shirt and still be a turkey." With that, the two of them put on shirts.

After a while, the sage signaled the servants again, and they threw him a pair of pants. Then he said to the prince, "What makes you think you can't be a turkey if you wear pants?"

The sage continued in this manner until they were both completely dressed.

Soon he signaled again, and he and the prince were given regular food from the table. Then the sage said, "What makes you think you will stop being a turkey if you eat good food? You can eat whatever you want and still be a turkey!" They both ate the food.

Finally, the sage said, "What makes you think a turkey must sit under a table? Even a turkey can sit at the table, and a turkey can also walk around anyplace it wants and no one objects."

The prince thought this through and accepted the wise man's opinion. Once he got up and walked about like a human being, he also began behaving like one.

This two-hundred-year-old fable illuminates some of the psychological dynamics involved in the process of change. We will refer to this fable again as we discuss these dynamics.[1]

Follow this amazingly simple six-step strategy to help anyone get rid of self-destructive habits or behaviors.

Psychological Component 1: One Thing at a Time, and One Thing Only

Once you begin the process of healing and eliminating self-destructive or self-defeating behaviors, the rest doesn't matter. Do not have a substance abuser, for example, try to change everything at

---

[1] Story by Rabbi Nachman of Breslov. Translated by Rabbi Aryeh Kaplan-ZAL. Contribution to psychological components by Rabbi Aryeh Leib Nivin.

once. Choose one area where you would like to see him make an improvement. Then begin to move him in a positive direction, all the while having his self-concept form itself around this successful, progressive image. The situation and dynamics of the relationship will best determine what you choose. If you want to start slowly, pick something gentle and less threatening—something, perhaps, that will make the person feel better about himself. Or you can go right to the heart of the matter and target precisely the self-destructive behavior that you want changed.

In the fable, the sage was moving along stage-by-stage while staying focused and one-dimensional. While he was getting the prince to wear clothing, the prince was still eating scraps off the floor. Even though that probably caused the sage distress, he kept his attention on the clothes and ignored the rest.

Whatever else the person you hope to change is doing matters not; you will give only positive reinforcement for positive behavior, and you will say nothing when he falls short in this area or any other. It doesn't matter what else is going on. Focus on one area and on building a new self-concept around his progress in this area.

EXAMPLE: *Your adult son Takeem is having trouble controlling his drinking.*

You could tackle Takeem's alcohol abuse first, or you could start with something related to his drinking that is more easily corrected. This could be anything from staying our of bars to keeping his home neat to getting to work on time. Whatever you pick, forget about the rest. Seek to make progress in one area only.

Be flexible in how you initially approach him. If you think Takeem will be fairly receptive, then let him know you want to help him get his life back on track, and say something like, "Son, let's work together on getting you cleaned up." But if you've got a tougher sell, then it is wise to lay the groundwork ahead of time to impart the seriousness of the situation. To do this, arrange a time to speak with him privately, and adopt a more serious tone. In both instances, what you say is much the same, but in this one be sure to communicate through your attitude that things must change.

Psychological Component 2: Begin Healing with an Instant Success

Why did the sage choose to have the prince put on a shirt first? After all, it's much worse to be without pants than without a shirt. The wise man understood a profound principle: when trying to change someone, begin with the easiest and most potentially successful step, something that will make the person feel good about himself—and then move from there. Once you get moving in the right direction, you will have momentum on your side, and the individual can begin to feel great with very little effort.

SIR ISAAC NEWTON

Sir Isaac Newton discovered that objects in motion tend to stay in motion, and objects at rest tend to stay at rest. He might as well have added that people in motion tend to stay in motion and people at rest tend to stay at rest. If you can get a person moving in the right direction, either physically or mentally, starting with something easy or perhaps for fun, you will being to generate positive momentum. The hardest thing to do is to begin. As the saying goes, a journey of a thousand miles begins with a single step. But once you are in motion, the laws of physics are engaged in your favor.

EXAMPLE: *Marcy wants to help her younger sister, Vicki, have more dignity.*

Marci wants Vicki to stop drinking all night and sleeping all day, but Marci has decided to focus on a smaller issue first: the condition of Vicki's apartment. If Vicki agrees to keep her home clean, then Vicki will not spend the entire day cleaning, vacuuming, and dusting. At first, Vicki will simply keep dishes from piling up in the sink, then move to keeping her clothes off the floor, and so on. While these might seem like inanely small steps, to Vicki, who doesn't care about herself or what she does, these steps are literally life-changing.

Psychological Component 3: Divide Healing into Doable Parts

Don't overwhelm the person you are trying to change! We saw in the turkey fable that there were at least five stages of healing: wearing the shirt, wearing the pants, being completely dressed, eating regular food, and then sitting at the table. Too often we make the mistake of trying to impart too much, too fast. When things are going well, there is a temptation to speed up the process. Be careful of this, or the person can burn out. It is almost always better to err on the side of moving too slowly.

EXAMPLE: *Stacy is trying to help her friend Bruce stop his binge eating.*

Whatever Bruce's goal, Stacy should divide it into bite-size pieces. He might move junk food out of his house. After a week, he could begin having a protein drink for breakfast; then he might begin a workout routine; and so on. Stacy must help him in stages, knowing that falling back may be part of the process. And she should go slowly, so that Bruce feels the success of his efforts and not the disappointment of his failures. She must avoid the temptation of moving too fast and having Bruce take on too much at one time.

Psychological Component 4: Consistency and Joy

It is important to stay the course, to be patient and joyful. Do not make the substance abuser, for example, feel as if he is your project or your job, something you hate to spend time on but feel you have to. Your relationship and his happiness is what matters to you, so let this come though. When things are difficult, let him know that it is still a pleasure to be with him, to have him in your life. He will feed off this. Avoid the temptation of judging and criticizing.

EXAMPLE: *You are helping your friend Martha get out of an abusive relationship.*

Smile when you are together. Let your joy come through, and say things such as, "This give us such a nice opportunity to spend time together. . . . I enjoy being with you, and helping you. . . . You are such a special person." Volunteer to do something together outside of the usual to show Martha that you enjoy being with her and that you're not simply hanging around to check up on things or because you'd feel guilty if you didn't.

Psychological Component 5: Unconditional Love

After the sage made himself indistinguishable from the turkey, he didn't try to heal him. He just spent time with him. An essential ingredient of healing is unconditional love or, when more appropriate, simple acceptance. That means, "I unconditionally love and/or respect you for who you are. Even if you never change, it is okay." Any relationship based on the need for one person to change will never succeed.

Many people constantly criticize the person they are trying to heal. But this is ineffective. The self-love becomes poisoned, and the unconditional love diluted. It requires tremendous focus, dedication, and patience to continually love and accept someone in the face of difficult behavior. Yet this is precisely what the sage did.

Understand that no one will change unless he or she likes who he/she is. The substance abuser does not have much self-respect. He gains it from you, and he must feel it from you in order to feel good about himself—to actually love himself. You don't harm or injure those you love, and so as the person begins to love himself, self-destructive behaviors lose their luster.

We cannot emphasize enough how important this is in the healing process. As Albert Schweitzer said, "Constant kindness can accomplish much. As the sun makes ice melt, kindness causes misunderstanding, mistrust, and hostility to evaporate."

ALL IN THE FAMILY

Your siblings and parents know you inside out. They know just about everything about you. And if they don't accept, respect, and love you, it can cause you—even if you are the most secure person in the world—to question your own self-worth. This is precisely why family members can get so angry at one another. We lash out because we are dependent to varying degrees on their approval.

EXAMPLE: *Jean is helping her husband, Ben, cut down on his drinking.*

How can Jean demonstrate unconditional love and acceptance? First, she can encourage Ben with positive words, feedback, and appreciation. She can be there to pick him up, not criticize him when he is down. She can let Ben know that she is there for him, no matter what he does, and that this will never change. She cannot say enough such phrases as, "You're doing great, and I will always be here for you, no matter how long it takes or how difficult it may become. I'm so proud of you for who you are, and nothing will ever change that."

Psychological Component 6: Simple Acceptance

Very often you can say and do everything right, but it's not good enough. Here's why: if your brother, for example, doesn't feel that you accepted him, everything you do will be filtered through this lens.

You must communicate that you do not think less of him for his beliefs, attitudes, values, career, and so on. It's okay though to disagree on fundamental ideas, while having respect for him and empathy for the struggles he may be going through.

This is important to understand. If there is a specific issue between the two of you, discuss it openly. Listen attentively and compassionately. Afterward, acknowledge that you see where he is coming from, and tell him you respect him for his position, not in spite of it.

EXAMPLE: *Ginger is helping her sister Colleen break a pattern of dating abusive men.*

Ginger should remind Colleen that she has great respect for who she is and how she conducts herself. Ginger should say something that conveys her respect, such as, "You know how much I value your opinion and trust your judgment." She should also let Ginger know, with genuine enthusiasm, how she marvels at something specific Ginger has done.

The situation will dictate what needs to be said. For instance, if a substance abuser's problem is drugs, you can say something like, "I want you to know that I think it's tremendous how you manage to keep moving forward with such a difficult addiction." Do not let him think that you look down on him, because then anything you say may be seen as condescending. But letting him know you respect him helps to put you on equal footing, so he is not only going to feel better about himself but more warmly to you as well.

Strategy Review

- Choose one—and only one—objective or area where you think a person can improve. Then begin to move him in a positive direction, all the while having his self-concept form around this successful, progressive image.
- As the saying goes, nothing succeeds like success. Begin the healing with an instant success.
- Divide the healing into bite-size chunks that the person is capable of doing. Don't overwhelm him with too much, too fast, as this will only make him shut down.
- It is important to stay the course, to be patient and joyful. Do not make the person feel as if he is your project, or a job you hate to do but feel you have to.
- An essential ingredient of healing is unconditional love. The love and appreciation of another person feeds our souls and recharges our emotional fuel tank.
- Accepting a person for who he is allows you not only to be closer, but it also gives him the security to be able to change.

See These Chapters for Additional Strategies:

⇨ Chapter 8: **A Quick-Fix Pick-Me-Up**
⇨ Chapter 9: **Give the Gift of Self-Esteem**
⇨ Chapter 11: **In Case of Emergency**
⇨ Chapter 23: **Make Anyone More Respectful**

In Case of Emergency

Emergency Technique 1: Back to Basics

Simplicity is a new trend in travel. Folks are trading four-star resorts for simple food, basic accommodation, and lots of hiking, walking, and exercising. Some of these programs charge several thousand dollars a week, and yet they are filled to capacity. Why? Because the world is getting so hectic, people need to turn off and connect to reality, to enjoy simple pleasures in a simple lifestyle.

While the author is not advocating the wholesale adoption of this lifestyle, it is interesting to note that the suicide rate among the Amish is fifty percent less than that of United States in general. And the incidence of drug and alcohol abuse among the Amish is less than one-third that of the general population. While the reasons are speculative, the absence of certain negative influences and the emphasis on a simple lifestyle and physical work surely play a role in the emotional stability of the Amish.

Many successful programs dealing with everyone from troubled teens to substance abusers understand the necessity of getting such people out of their environment in order to change their behavior. Additionally, engaging in physical labor helps to get them outside their heads and thus allows them to reconnect with the world in a whole new way.

EXAMPLE: *A grandfather is helping his granddaughter, Beth, to quit drugs and get out of a gang.*

If the grandfather is not making much progress or feels that he has a tough case to begin with, then getting Beth to a new place physically will more easily get her to a new place emotionally. Moreover, getting Beth back to basics and engaging in physical activity—whether it is mowing lawns, cooking, or planting a garden—allows her to see with her own eyes that her actions have consequences.

Another option is to have her sign up for the Peace Corps, the army reserve, or any other regimented program. At the very least, even a couple of weeks away doing structured activity will allow Beth to more easily make progress.

Emergency Technique 2: Want into Need

You do not have to motivate a mother bird to build a nest, nor give her a seminar on Effective Time Management for the Busy Bird. She simply does it. It's not a question of fitting nest building into her schedule. Things like procrastination or lack of discipline do not enter into the equation. It is a matter of need, not of motivation.

Technique 2 raises the level of what you want someone to do into a need. This means that by not doing what you want him to do, he cannot just simply revert back to how things were. Everything changes. These is no more business as usual.

If you arrange it so that he will lose something from engaging in the behavior, then you greatly increase his chances of compliance. For instance, how often do we hear about a man finally shaping up after an ultimatum is issued? Impetus for action is often created when he is threatened with the loss of his job or wife. Some people need to push the envelope of life until it pushes back.

Let the person know in clear and simple terms the consequences of his behavior, that he will lose what he has if he continues to engage in self-destructive, unhealthy behavior.

We don't appreciate what we take for granted, and this person may need to be reminded what is at stake. The effective advice a woman employs with her noncommittal boyfriend is, in fact, to issue an ultimatum: either marriage or the door. This usually shakes up the man, forcing him to make a decision. While some men choose the door, at least the woman is no longer wasting her time. And so you must be prepared to follow through on what you say.

Emergency Technique 2 is about "tough love." And in the right circumstances, it is highly effective. As discussed in the previous chapter, unconditional love should always be used in conjunction with the other components, but if you have already pursued that course and exhausted its potential, then this technique offers an effective supplement.

EXAMPLE: *Fran wants her son Dan to stop hanging around with a bad crowd.*

Fran threatens Dan—and then she follows through, if need be—to stop all support, financial and otherwise, that she is giving him. She uses whatever leverage she has to bargain with. Then she draws a line in the sand, and if he crosses it, she takes action.

It is still important for Fran to stay the course, to be patient and joyful. As mentioned earlier an essential ingredient of healing is unconditional love. The love and appreciation she shows feed her son emotionally, and allow him to grow in a healthier direction. She should never take this away.

Plastic Surgery for the Personality

*Discover the Psychological Principles
That Can Rechannel a Person's
Personality, Nature, and Character.
Turn That Annoying, Arrogant, Lazy,
Self-centered, Self-absorbed Person into
a Giving, Kind, and Easygoing Pleasure.*

Nothing endures but change.

—HERACLITUS (540–480 B.C.)

Chapter 12

Can You Really Change a Person's Personality?

At one time or another have you ever acted out of character and afterward felt great about yourself? Being a certain "type" of person is not a matter of having it *in* you, it's a matter of bringing it *out*.

We human beings are driven to act in accordance with how we see ourselves. Like a rubber band, we will stretch only so far before snapping back into our original position.

Information is only part of the equation. The real question is, How do we see ourselves? We often think that change is merely about doing what makes sense. But people do not necessarily do what makes sense. Diet and exercise are important, yet 65 percent of Americans are overweight. Family is what matters most, yet everyone knows a relative who is not talking to somebody else in the family. Statistically, you are safer in an airplane than you are in a car. And yet, the same person who thinks nothing of driving to work turns white at the thought of flying.

The psychological techniques in this section show how to

quickly and dramatically reshape a person's personality by changing the way he sees himself.

ON A ROLL

Have you ever experienced the incredible "on a roll" phenomenon where absolutely nothing gets in your way, you're unstoppable, and you succeed at everything you try? And then there are times when nothing goes right, everything you touch goes wrong, and you're afraid to even get out of bed. What is it that causes us to get carried along on such streaks? Fascinating research shows that a streak is caused by the way in which our transitional self-concept has been shaped around unfolding events. We see ourselves as that kind of person, and hence we perform in a consistent manner. Even events seemingly beyond our complete control can be subject to this law.

Chapter 13

Change Anyone's Mind, and Stop Stubborn Behavior Anytime

At home or at work, it's "his way or the highway," and you've had enough. If you're tired of dealing with someone who refuses to see the facts, the five psychological techniques in this chapter can help you to make him more flexible and more open-minded to what you have to say.

Technique 1: The Crowbar

The crowbar technique, borrowed from my book *Never Be Lied to Again*, helps you to get a person to begin to think about the possibility of believing differently.

EXAMPLE: *You want your friend Sheila to hear you out on new idea, and she is adamantly opposed to listening to you.*

Tell Sheila that you want her to agree to think about, listen to, or read certain information, but only if *you* can achieve some highly difficult and amazing task. For instance, you tell Sheila to write down on a piece of paper a number from one to one hundred. If you can guess what it is, then she will agree to what you want. She will likely agree because she believes that there is little chance that you will guess the number.

The psychological strategy here is not about being right, but about Sheila's agreeing to take the chance. In getting her to agree, you manage to slightly adjust her belief system—and this is all that you need. You take her from a no to a maybe.

Only someone who would, in the back of her mind, be willing to take your advice would agree to this test. So some part of Sheila, to some degree, is willing. Now you also know that you are not dealing with an impossible person, and now she will have to alter her belief system to allow the possibility—though remote—that what you have to say may make sense. In order to reduce dissonance, Sheila unconsciously adjusts her thinking and will now become more open.

Technique 2: Saving Face

Whenever possible, it is important to lessen the blow a bit, as it were. A person needs to be able to deflect a direct hit to his ego and justify to himself (and possibly others) his belief up until now. He needs a plausible explanation to the question, Why did I believe something for so long if it is not true?

Studies show that if a person can point to an outside influence, he can retroactively justify his behavior. The emotional pain of trying to reconcile a false belief dissipates when he can release the pressure by attributing behavior to something other than his own desire.

For example, let's say Jim shaved his head and gave up his money, friends, and lifestyle to join a cult. He thinks that he has either done the most idiotic thing in the world or the cult is a great idea. This dissonance, this pressure, most often is released by taking the easiest, least painful way out. And so Jim concludes that he made a wise choice, and he bides his time, waiting for the spaceship to arrive. However, if a gun was put to his head and he was forced to join, then the internal pressure is released by this external cause. Simply, he does not have to assume responsibility only to then justify his behavior.

Now the obvious question is, How do you create an external cause after the fact? It is done through information—that is, by giving Jim new knowledge about an old decision. A person will not hold himself responsible for making a wrong turn in the dark. If he could see, that's one thing, but choosing left or right when he cannot see is not really a choice in the first place. So the internal pressure to justify his behavior is greatly released by giving the ego the opportunity to consider that he did the best he could, given the information available. But now, in light of additional information, he admits that a different conclusion makes more sense.

EXAMPLE: *You want Clark to rethink his support for the death penalty.*

You might say, "It turns out that with DNA testing up to ten percent of the people on death row are innocent. I know you would never be a party to the killing of ten innocent persons in the course of executing ninety guilty people. We never would have known this without the new technology, so you would have no way of knowing that this was going on." You would explain further that many people are wrongly convicted and that the system may be inherently flawed, with a disproportionate number of the poor and minority groups being convicted.

In the interest of balance, let us take the opposing view to see how this technique is applied. You might say, "I understand why you were against capital punishment for so long. Although now, studies show something that we never knew before. And that is that victims' families are able to move on with their lives and heal faster when the person who killed their loved one is put to death. And did you know that the amount of money it takes to keep a prisoner in a cell for the rest of his life could actually save 2.4 lives if that same money was spent on crime prevention? So you're actually saving more lives through capital punishment."

AVOIDING REACTANCE

You must satisfy the unasked question a person is thinking: why are you trying to change my mind? *Reactance theory* states that people may do the opposite of what you want them to do if they believe you are trying to get them to change their mind. This problem is bypassed if they understand and believe that while this is true, you have their best interests at heart, not simply your own.

Technique 3: Quantify

Beliefs are usually expressed as absolutes, in black and white. "I can do this," "I believe . . . ," "I like . . . ," and so on. In an abstract whirl, sometimes devoid of logic or reason, it is nearly impossible to argue because you cannot get any traction. To change a person's thinking, you first need to get him to define exactly what he means.

This is precisely what skilled trial attorneys do when questioning opposing witnesses. They seek to quantify statements and then pick them apart. Let's look at the following dialogue between plaintiff and defense attorney:

PLAINTIFF: "I was a hard worker."

ATTORNEY: "What do you mean by 'hard worker'?"

PLAINTIFF: "I worked late at night and on weekends."

ATTORNEY: "Every night and every weekend?"

PLAINTIFF: "Well, no. Most."

ATTORNEY: "How many nights a week?"

PLAINTIFF: "Three or four."

ATTORNEY: "Consistently? Or were there some weeks that you didn't work late?"

PLAINTIFF: "Well, around the holidays, I was off early."

ATTORNEY: "So you not only didn't work late, but you took off early. And isn't it true that you took five sick days?"

If the lawyer didn't seek to quantify what the witness meant by "hard worker," he would not be able to poke holes in his statement. You can only take something apart that has parts. When someone presents an attitude, you must seek to break it down or its rationale and truthfulness cannot be questioned. But if you can quantify it, then you can pick it apart.

EXAMPLE: *Your friend Regina thinks vitamins don't work and are a waste of money.*

To get Regina to be more open-minded, use one of the following questions. They are effective in beginning the process of quantifying a statement.

- *"What evidence would convince you that vitamins do work?"*
- *"If someone you really respect took vitamins, would that change your mind?"*
- *"When you say, 'vitamins don't work,' do you mean all vitamins?"*

- *"When you say, 'vitamins don't work,' do you mean that 90 percent of them pass through a person and only a small amount is absorbed?"*
- *"Why do you believe this is true?"*

Technique 4: Reciprocal Persuasion

A study by psychologist Robert Cialdini found that if you persuade someone to change his attitude toward an idea—for example, trying a new sales approach, testing a new recipe, or test-driving a new car—you are more inclined to change your own thinking about one of his ideas. If he was previously resistant and then you get him to agree with your thinking, you are then unconsciously driven to reciprocate and be more receptive to an idea he presents to you.

In Technique 4, however, *you* are the one who has a change of heart about something a person suggests. And when you adopt his thinking, he becomes more open to what you have to say. In addition to invoking the law of *reciprocal persuasion*, you do another very powerful thing: by agreeing with his opinion, you show that you trust his judgment and value his input. This helps you to gain his support when you want him to rethink his beliefs.

EXAMPLE: *You want your boss, Richard, to listen to your new idea.*

Saying something like, "I thought about what you said regarding (a previous conversation where he was explaining his point of view), and I've come to agree with your thinking. You're right." This makes you more credible in Richard's mind because if you took his advice, then you must be a smart person. Thus he's even more open to what you have to say. A day or so later, reintroduce your idea to him. Be sure to offer a little new information, so that he feels like he's making a new decision based on new information, not simply changing his mind: "Richard, I'd like to show you some new statistics that may convince us to adopt a new marketing strategy."

Technique 5: Okay, You're Right, but Do It My Way Anyway.

Instead of making an issue about right or wrong, simply ask Richard to do it as a favor. Now he will feel as if he's doing something nice — a favor for you — as opposed to giving in. This completely changes the psychological dynamics, because he can still be right and do what you want anyway.

By trying to get Richard to change his mind, you have two obstacles: the ego and the intellect. So instead, by asking him to do what you want, even though he does not agree, you avoid engaging his ego. You are not telling him he is wrong, and so he does not have to defend his position. Therefore, you eliminate the gatekeeper, and the intellect can now clearly and objectively consider if Richard can agree to your request.

EXAMPLE: *You and your husband disagree over whether you should go back to work.*

Offer a brief, reasonable case as to why your husband's thinking does not make sense to you; do not argue. Simply say the following:

- You have thought about what he wants, and you appreciate how he feels about it.
- You understand that he doesn't agree with your returning to work and that he feels he is right, but you would like him to go along with your way of thinking anyway. As a favor to you. Not because you have convinced him he is wrong, but rather because it is important for you to try to return to work.

- You will stop working, without hesitation or conversation, if it becomes clear that it is not working.

By eliminating the power struggle and not arguing over right and wrong, you are putting your husband in a position of power, and this is what he likely craves.

Strategy Review

- When a person does not want to think about, listen to, or do what you ask, ask him if he will do so if you can achieve some highly difficult and amazing task. If he does agree, then you've managed to loosen his belief system slightly — and this is all you need.
- Soften the blow to a person's ego by providing a plausible justification for his thinking. In this way it is not shown that he was wrong, but rather that the information leading to his belief was faulty.
- To change a person's position, break it down into quantifiable parts. This allows you to take his thinking apart with great precision and ease.
- If you take a person's advice on something, he becomes more likely to listen to what you have to say (this illustrates the psychological *law of reciprocation*).
- Instead of twisting someone's arm to see your side of things, simply agree that he may be right, but ask him to listen to you anyway.

See These Chapters for Additional Srategies:
⇨ Chapter 5: **Eliminate Prejudice in Anyone**
⇨ Chapter 8: **A Quick-Fix Pick-Me-Up**
⇨ Chapter 9: **Give the Gift of Self-Esteem**

Chapter 14

Make Anyone More Assertive

It's been fifteen minutes, and the server hasn't come over to Eleanor's table. Although she's starving, she doesn't want to make scene. And Eleanor's newspaper is always late and wet, the next-door neighbor has his camper parked half on her lawn, and the supermarket cashier rang up the wrong price. But Eleanor does nothing about it.

Use the following techniques to instill in people like Eleanor an unwavering ability to stand up for themselves and for what they believe is right.

Technique 1: Expanding Definition

For better or worse we all see ourselves in a certain way. And while this way may include negative behaviors or traits, it is nonetheless who we are. And being true to ourself is often more important to us than is being better than who we are.

Change can be very scary. So with Technique 1 you do not try to change a person per se; rather you change the definition of what his self-concept includes. This allows the person to act differently while still seeing himself as he always has been.

EXAMPLE: *You want your "never wants to make waves" friend, Joanne, to be more assertive.*

For instance, at a restaurant you might say, "Just because you are shy doesn't mean you should be treated like a second-class citizen. Don't let the waitress ignore you. Shy people still have rights." You are not telling Joanne not to be shy; rather, you are saying that even shy people can speak up every once in a while.

Another application of this psychology is to ask Joanne to simply try something once. Let her know that she can always go back to her old self and her old way of doing things whenever she wants. In this way she has the comfort of a home base and never has to feel in emotional limbo. She is not committing herself to anything, and so she has no fear of being someone new. To go this route you might say, "Just this one time tell the waiter you want the menu, and if you never want to ask again, you don't have to."

Technique 2: Image Adjustment

One of a stutterer's greatest fears is the phone. It rings; he tenses up. To change his self-concept, you have to break patterns associated with old way of seeing himself and reshape how he sees himself in this situation. Even with intense therapy—and the ability to speak fluently in some situations—if a person still *sees* himself as someone who stutters and has a negative association to a ringing phone, he will snap right back into that old pattern and freeze as soon as the phone rings.

To reset his image, the stutterer needs a new association. To break this pattern, you do an exercise in which the phone rings, he smiles, and that's it! Fifty times, and then again. Then in the next set, the phone rings, and he smiles and walks over, briskly and confidently. After several more times he picks up the phone with commanding confidence and says a booming "hello" while smiling.

The stutterer now has a powerful new image of himself. It is an image whereby he doesn't have to force himself to conjure up a relaxed, powerful, and in-control self-image. Instead we have diluted the old concept so that the new self is representative of how he automatically sees himself. Now when the phone rings, he is reminded more readily of this self-concept than the old one.

Technique 2 also helps to establish self-efficacy, as well as a new anchor for an instant association. As you will see with the next technique, a person's expectation of performance greatly affects his *actual* performance.

PHOBIAS

Self-efficacy affects how a person deals with a phobia. Research shows that through systematic desensitization—for example, where a person who has a fear of snakes is exposed first to a picture, then a toy snake, then a real one behind glass, and so on —efficacy increased and so too did the person's ability to handle the situation. Simply, he saw himself as not "freaking out" with each small step, and so he remained calm for the subsequent step. In time, the phobia was diluted (Bandura, A., & Adams, N. E. 1977).

This type of behavioral modification is a great way to get unassertive people used to, and comfortable with, moving outside their zone of comfort. Continuously engaging in behavior that is a stark contrast to their usual manner allows you to dilute this old self-image and replace it with a newer, more assertive picture in their mind.

EXAMPLE: *Your shy friend Samantha has trouble introducing her-self to new people.*

Have Samantha "introduce" herself to you in a safe nonthreatening environment. Have her repeat the same phrase time and time again: "Hi, my name is Samantha. It's nice to meet you." After she does this several hundred times, move to the real world—for example, a cocktail party. Then have Samantha introduce herself to as many people as she can. After simply saying, "Hello, how are you?" over and over within a short period of time, her very nature will begin to undergo a transformation.

Technique 3: Self-Efficacy and Feedback

How we respond to a situation, from public speaking to phobias, is based largely upon our expectation of performance. Simply, if we believe we'll do okay, then we likely will. Studies show that even when feedback from others is false and our performance does not measure up, it still increases our level of confidence and performance in subsequent trials. The opposite is also true: negative feedback produces a fall-off in performance.

Ever since we were young, our input has been controlled by our parents, teachers, friends, the culture, religion, and so on. The unconscious brain is fed with millions of messages that probably began when we were in the womb. How many youngsters growing up in inner cities heard their parents repeatedly say, "You'll end up dead or in jail"? And sure enough, they ended up dead or in jail. The brain is a computer, and whatever you feed in, comes out.

EXAMPLE: *You are helping your young cousin, Marissa, be more assertive.*

Do not ever criticize Marissa's poor performance. How she feels she is doing will affect her future behavior and performance. And her beliefs about her ability to perform hinge greatly on your behavior. Whenever Marissa acts assertively, praise her lavishly, and regardless of actual performance. And be supportive when she falls short.

WHAT'S IN A NAME?

What you call a person can greatly influence how he behaves. Thus a name like Stinky or Pinky is not such a great idea. When you want someone to take on a new persona, encourage him to go by a new nickname or his full name, whichever he is not currently using. Let the name convey a sense of self-respect.

Technique 4: Instant Immersion

Behavioral change can come about in one of two ways: by a slow progressive journey or a radical leap. When change is more dramatic, it almost always occurs in conjunction with the person taking a huge step, a significant action. In Technique 4, you pretty much do whatever you can to get the person in the right state of mind to take the proverbial plunge. Such a huge step forces him to shift his perspective because he now sees himself as an entirely different kind of person. In addition he will often find that the experience is not nearly as difficult or painful as he had imagined.

EXAMPLE: *A father wants his young son, Jimmy, to play with other kids.*

The father might say, "Jimmy, if you go over and play with those boys I'll take you out for lunch and you can order anything you want. You don't even have to have a good time. Just throw the ball around for five minutes, and then you're done." This takes the pressure off Jimmy and offers him a needed incentive. Because a child would normally play with others for fun, by removing fun and replacing it with something that he's guaranteed, it makes it easier for him to take the plunge. This accomplishes more than a short-term gain. The father slowly reshapes Jimmy's self-image around his new assertive behavior and gets him in the habit of acting this way.

Technique 5: The Reality of Illusions

James Nesmeth, a prisoner of war in Vietnam for seven years, maintained his sanity by playing a game of golf in his head every day. All eighteen holes. So real was his visualization that it took just about as long to finish his mental game as it does a real game. He imagined the trees and grass on the golf course, how the club felt in his hand, and so on. What's most amazing is that when he was released and played his first real game of golf, his score improved from the low 90s to the low 70s. The power of the imagination is enormous. Used productively, it can transform a person's life for the better.

EXAMPLE: *A teacher wants Hillary, one of her young students, to be more assertive.*

The teacher has the girl rehearse in her head acting assertively in a variety of situations. For instance, "Hillary, I want you to imagine that you're in the cafeteria, and Caroline takes your seat. See yourself politely telling Caroline that you were sitting there, and then see her apologizing and getting up." The teacher can have Hillary cycle through different scenarios where she stands up for herself and is successful. In a short time she will begin to see herself this way, and to act in accordance with the same confidence she rehearsed.

Strategy Review

- In helping someone be more assertive, expand the definition of what it means to be unassertive. Then the person's not abandoning his self-concept when taking a courageous action.
- You can reset a person's self-image through a process of anchors and triggers. By changing a person's association with certain stimuli, his self-concept can be reshaped to fall in line.
- How someone responds to a situation, from public speaking to phobias, is based largely upon expectation of performance. This is shaped largely by the feedback he gets from others. Be positive and encouraging about his subsequent efforts.
- Offer an external reward—a bribe—to get a person to take action. In time, he will be able to act assertively, even when the added impetus is removed.
- Use the power of visualization to transform how a person not only thinks, but behaves.

See These Chapters for Additional Strategies:

⇨ Chapter 15: **Turn a Lazy Bum into an Ambitious Go-Getter**
⇨ Chapter 18: **Turn Any Wallflower Into a Social Butterfly**

Turn a Lazy Bum into an Ambitious Go-Getter

She just sits on the couch all day watching TV. She doesn't seem to have any goals or desire to do anything. She's smart, but completely unmotivated. In the past she's broken out of this groove from time to time, but never with any sustained effort. If this describes someone you know, then use the following techniques to turn the lazy bum into an ambitious go-getter.

YOU ARE GETTING SLEEEEEPY!

You can use the power of words to greatly influence a person's behavior. One study showed that after being exposed to words related to the elderly such as *old*, *grey*, and *bingo*, participants walked away 15 percent more slowly than did those exposed to neutral words (Bargh et al. 1996). Pepper conversations with words like *passionate*, *exciting*, and *fired-up*, and you will fuel a person's thirst for taking action.

Technique 1: Structure and Focus

Too many options can paralyze us into inaction. None of us enjoy being wrong or second-guessing ourselves at every corner. So fewer choices mean we will make a decision faster and be less likely to dwell on it afterward.

Children who grow up without a sense of structure often have great difficulty managing their lives as adults. *Lack of structure does not free us; it paralyzes us.* Structure provides the framework for us to move, hopefully in a meaningful direction. Have you ever heard it said, If you want something done, give it to a busy person? Why? Because busy people are moving.

Every major religion dictates a code of conduct, specifying things you can do, and things you cannot do. This illustrates that the need for human beings to have boundaries and borders is necessary to their emotional well-being. And someone who does not feel in control needs a sense of structure most of all. It is interesting to note that the Hebrew prayer book itself is called the "siddur," which means order.

There are more than enough unqualified geniuses who sit around and do nothing. These talented folks either end up dabbling in a hundred directions and move nowhere or are paralyzed by the fear of moving in any direction. Such people need emotional blinders to keep them focused in one direction at one time.

EXAMPLE: *Margaret wants her son, Micah, to excel as a freelance artist.*

Margaret needs to help Micah organize to avoid feeling overwhelmed. His long-term goal should be broken down into months, then weeks, then days. And on his daily "to do" list should be at least one thing that absolutely needs to get done. After Micah accomplishes this objective, he can move further down the list.

Additionally, Margaret should help him come up with a routine that gives his life a semblance of order. It should not be rigid and difficult, but rather frame his day with structure while allowing some flexibility. Ideally, Micah's day should include a set time when he does things that he doesn't enjoy doing, but really needs to do—and the earlier in the day, the better. He will feel good about himself for having gotten those tasks behind him, and he will be in a better mood throughout the rest of the day.

Technique 2: Force a Deadline

Giving a deadline for action fulfills two important psychological motivations. First, a task will expand or contract depending upon how much time we allow for it. The world operates on deadlines and expiration dates. Without an immediate need to move forward, most people will not. It is human nature to postpone action until conditions become more favorable, until we have more information, or until we are in a better mood. Second, we don't like our freedom to be restricted. Whenever we are told we cannot have—or do—something, we often end up desiring it more. So by letting an individual know that he or she may not get the opportunity to act in the future, you create an incentive for him to move now.

Be imaginative in applying this rule of human behavior. For example, let the person know that there is a deadline or expiration date, or that someone else is competing for the same opportunity, or that the offer will be withdrawn at a certain time. Try anything from reminding him that the maximum opportunity to act is passing him by to orchestrating behind the scenes to close the window of opportunity—and then watch him jump off the couch.

EXAMPLE: *An architectural firm wants its building partner to stop dragging its feet, make a decision on a building design, and begin construction.*

To apply this technique, the firm could inform the builders that unless they make a decision by a certain date, it will have to start work with another client: "George, you know we'd love to work with you, so please get back to me by the fifth. Otherwise, it will be about two years before we can revisit this project together." By the way, if George says he does not want to go ahead, the firm has just saved itself a lot of time, money, and heartache.

Technique 3: The Power of Recall

Fascinating studies of memory and behavior conclude that people often base their self-concept on availability, or how easily they can bring information to mind. For instance, if you were asked to think of several times when you acted ambitiously and were able to recall these events with relative ease, then you would think of yourself as ambitious. Conversely, if you could not come up with an example, then you would conclude that you were cautious and conservative.

Of course, we can say, for example, that a woman cannot come up with such examples because this is the way she is. However, studies show that even when these memories are few and far between, as in the case of the woman who is not ambitious, if she rehearses recalling them so they are easily brought to mind, she will then see herself as more ambitious.

EXAMPLE: *Harvey is helping his brother Ken to be more ambitious.*

Harvey asks Ken to review several times daily occasions in the past when he acted ambitiously. This facilitates the ease of recall and allows Ken's self-concept to mold itself around this image. For instance, Harvey could say, "Ken, can you tell me about the last time you found yourself doing something really ambitious? Wow, you made reservations to go to Italy and then gave yourself just six weeks to learn the language? Okay. What else? You just walked into a place that was hiring and asked for a job? Great. How did that feel? And can you tell me about the time before that? And the time before that?" Harvey then instructs Ken to review these occasions vividly several times daily. As the weeks and months go by, newer, more vivid, ambitious behaviors take the place of previous ones.

Technique 4: A Very Narrow Bridge

We will work for something, enduring a great deal of pain and sacrifice, if we really want it. Through the power of psychology we can influence someone's perception, magnifying his desire and making him want something more.

It is human nature to want what we cannot have and to want more of what we have to work for. More than just limiting his options or providing a deadline, the less choice a person has, the less clearly he sees what is available to him. He gives greater importance and prominence to what is left. For instance, a person with several job offers is likely to see and evaluate each offer with great objective diligence. A person who has been unemployed for two years, with a stack of bills on his kitchen table, who finally lands a job interview, will go over it again and again, thinking about it nonstop, dwelling on every scrap of minutiae, filled with fear that he may not get the job. He is obsessed, but only because his options are limited. The odds of getting the job are the same, but his perspective forces him to be less confident and more concerned.

The narrowing of options forces human beings to hypermagnify what is available to them, creating a skewed perspective, forcing them to run toward what is still left.

EXAMPLE: *Judy, a talent agent, wants her client Joey to take an acting job he's not thrilled about.*

Judy could say, "You know, Joey, if you don't take this job, the client is not going to offer you another job. You may not like this one, but it's the only way to get better parts." Now the equation isn't simply take the job or not. Rather it is take the job or have no future whatsoever in the business. Different equation, whole new attitude. Judy might also say, "This can be a breakthrough role. Jobs like this come along once in a career. I know you still want to think it over, but I just hope the offer is still on the table when you decide."

Technique 5: A Zest for Life

A person's lack of ambition may actually be a lack of passion for how he spends his days. Sometimes a person is not moving because he is not interested in where he is going. So help him to examine his priorities and goals in life. Once he's honest with himself, he can move ahead more genuinely and sincerely.

When someone appears to be unmotivated or lazy, what he really is uninspired. He needs to feel joy in what he is doing so that the pleasure of doing something is greater than the pleasure of doing nothing.

EXAMPLE: A *father wants his twenty-five-year-old son to get a job and move out of the house.*

The father should ask his son to think about what he enjoys doing and what he is good at. Somewhere in between he will find something that truly inspires him. For instance, if he enjoys computers and video games, he may find writing codes for video games to be rewarding. Or if he enjoys working with people and is a talented musician, he might give classes to aspiring musicians.

Once the son is clear on what he wants to do, the father should have him move every so slightly in that direction. The father will find that once his son begins moving, he will be more willing to be proactive in other areas of his life, and he will accomplish that which he has previously ignored or been procrastinating about. If the father is able to, he should help his son in whatever way necessary to move in this positive direction.

Technique 6: You Are What You Wear

Whatever we care about, we care *for*. An interesting psychological phenomenon exists whereby the mere act of treating something or someone better makes us like it or the person more. Therefore in the father-son example, the father should encourage his son to treat himself with greater respect. Mostly unconsciously, it will increase his appreciation for himself. This in turn will increase his desire to do something with himself and his life. Whenever we invest ourselves in anything—giving our time, energy, attention—we feel more lovingly toward it.

APPEARANCE

Have you ever noticed that your mood changes depending upon the clothes you wear? The effect of clothing has been shown in numerous studies to influence, sometimes significantly, our attitudes and behavior. For instance, a "mock prison" experiment showed that men who merely donned guard uniforms became more aggressive, while those playing the role of prisoner and wearing prisoner garb became passive and more reclusive (Haney et al. 1973). Dress-down

Fridays, all the rage a few years back, have now been abandoned by many companies after the discovery that employee productivity often slipped on those days. Clothing is more than a reflection of who we are; it has the potential to affect *how* we are.

ENVIRONMENT

If you don't treat your belongings and surroundings with respect, then you are sending a message that says, it doesn't matter how I live. When you treat anyone or anything as worthless, you also come to regard it as so. Remember that respect and love go hand in hand. This is true for objects and things as well as for people. Taking care of his environment is a good way to motivate a person to take care of himself.

EXAMPLE: *As a therapist you want your client Pedro to be more ambitious.*

You should encourage Pedro to dress in neat, clean, and appropriate clothes. You might have him sort through his wardrobe, and give away what is no longer appropriate. Helping him coordinate what he wears or having him learn a bit about fashion basics may help to spark his interest.

Please understand that we are not emphasizing appearance for its own sake. Instead, we are talking about a man presenting himself in a dignified way, where the external reflects a sense of inner confidence and self-worth.

Also, encourage Pedro to have a neat and clean environment. To accomplish this, have him get as organized as possible, and to throw out or store things he does not use.

Strategy Review

- No structure and too many options can paralyze a person into inaction. To avoid the feeling of being overwhelmed, he should prioritize by deciding what is the one thing he absolutely needs to get done today. Then he should focus his energies on that.

- A task will expand or contract depending upon how much time we allow for it. If there is no immediate need for people to move forward, most of them will not do so. In some way try to make them aware that their options will not always be available to them.

- Ask the person to review several times daily—in his mind, out loud, on paper—those occasions when he acted ambitiously. This facilitates an ease of recall and allows for his self-concept to mold itself around this image.

- By narrowing a person's perspective, you artificially magnify the importance of what is available to him. With no other options, his desire is increased dramatically.

- A person has to be excited about the direction in which he is moving. Make sure no conflicting values are holding him back.

- By getting a person to improve his appearance and environment, you help him gain a greater sense of self-respect. As a result, he will be more inclined to invest in his future and in himself.

See These Chapters for Additional Strategies:

⇨ Chapter 8: **A Quick-Fix Pick-Me-Up**
⇨ Chapter 9: **Give the Gift of Self-Esteem**
⇨ Chapter 18: **Turn Any Wallflower into a Social Butterfly**
⇨ Chapter 26: **Make Anyone More Interested in Anything**

Chapter 16

Silence the Gossipmonger in Anyone

There is nothing Anna enjoys more than spreading a little news around the watercooler. She gets right on the phone to tell someone the "latest," and she's excited when she has an opportunity to share some "dirt"—and she does so every chance she gets.

While most people are guilty of this pastime every once in a while, there are those who thrive on gossip. If Anna lives to tell people the latest, she does so for one or more of the following reasons: (1) the misdeeds of others offer her an opportunity to feel better about her own conduct; (2) by discussing the lives of other people, she doesn't have to face the perils in her own life; and (3) gossiping gives her a sense of power. She knows something that somebody else doesn't. Others will come to her for information, giving her a feeling of prestige and importance.

Regardless of the reasons, you can put an end to anyone's gossiping by using the following psychological strategy.

Technique 1: Let Go My Ego

You want to change Anna's definition of what it means to be in control and to have power. If Anna comes to understand that the one who keeps a secret is the one who is liked and respected, and the one who cannot keep her mouth shut is the one nobody likes, then the ego-boomerang effect occurs. The very force that moved Anna to gossip is the same one that now moves her not to.

Anna gossips because she *thinks* it gains her respect and admiration. But if she discovers that the very thing she seeks is obtained through not gossiping, then she will reverse course.

EXAMPLE: *You want your assistant, Samantha, to keep rumors to herself.*

You, and anyone you care to enlist, should talk openly, saying, for example, "Barbara is terrific because she is someone who knows how to keep things to herself. I love that she will change the subject if anyone is speaking negatively about another person. She doesn't get caught up in the whole gossip game. I know I can trust her with anything. She's great." Now Samantha also wants to be great. And so she will mimic what Barbara does to gain praise and adulation, and leave her gossiping ways behind.

Technique 2: Internal Momentum

Studies show that if you get Samantha to agree to your way of thinking, simply by affirming what you say, then emotionally she will have a difficult time going against what she just declared to be true. As we have stated, human beings need consistency between thought and action. Once she declares her disdain for gossiping, Samantha will be unconsciously "blocked" from engaging in the same behavior.

EXAMPLE: *Deena wants to curb her mother-in-law's gossiping.*

Deena might say, "Don't you think that a person appreciates it when she's not talked about? Don't you think that people who gossip do it just to make themselves feel more important?" Her mother-in-law will then offer some sort of agreement. And that's it.

This is effective because human beings have a need to act in accordance with our attitudes. And once Deena's mother-in-law expresses agreement with her statement, she will have a hard time deviating from it.

Technique 3: Will the Real Story Please Stand Up?

When we understand why a person gossips, we see that his own credibility—the ability to deliver interesting and truthful tidbits—is crucial. So if you "feed" him many crazy false stories, he won't know what to believe, and when he spreads them around, he will eventually be as interesting as a newspaper that reports celebrities giving birth to two-headed chickens.

Technique 3 works like a viral infection. Once it gets into a person, he spreads it himself, and with each word he utters, he continues to damage his own reputation. Of course, you don't want to be guilty of gossiping yourself, so tell him rumors that are clearly absurd—but not about any person in particular.

EXAMPLE: *Nora wants a coworker, Nick, to stop gossiping about her.*

Every morning Nora should say things like, "Nick, did you hear that a guy in a gorilla suit broke into the building last night?" and "Nick, I just found out that our company is being bought out by the Chinese, and anyone who can't speak Chinese in six months will be fired," or "Nick, I heard that, to save money, we have to work with half the lights off." This technique works well because even if Nick does not believe these stories, he will come to understand the lunacy in spreading rumors of any sort.

Technique 4: See How It Feels

Technique 4 gives a gossiper a taste of his own medicine. You, and anyone else you wish to enlist, inform him that you heard something about him. However, you will not repeat it because it is wrong to do so.

Often someone who gossips about others has not really thought about the damage he is doing. This technique helps the person to feel, in a very real way, the damage he causes. But there's one other twist to the technique that creates a triple bind, as you will see in the following.

EXAMPLE: *At camp, a couple of girls want Terri to stop gossiping.*

One or more of the girls should say something like, "Terri, I want you to know I heard a rumor about you, but rest assured I would never repeat it to anyone." Terri will, of course, be curious about two things: where the girl(s) heard it from and what the rumor is. The response is, "I overheard it from someone—I really don't know who—and the rumor is that people think that you are the biggest gossiper on the planet." This creates a powerful threefold incentive for Terri to discontinue her ways.

When Terri learns that the rumor is the fact that she gossips, she cannot really deny it; second, she feels bad that people are talking about her, and so she understands the pain that she has been causing; and third, to put an end to everyone's gossiping about her, Terri has to stop herself.

Strategy Review

- Reshape a person's definition of what it means to be in control and have power. If he understands that the one who can keep a secret is the one who is liked and respected, and the one who cannot keep his mouth shut is the one who nobody likes, then the ego-boomerang effect occurs.
- If you can get someone to make a statement consistent with a new belief, then he will have a hard time going against what he too proclaimed to be true.
- Introduce absurd rumors into the rumor mill, and a gossiper won't know what is true and what is not. Eventually he will tire of the gossip game, and he will not be taken seriously when he does try to spread rumors.
- Put the shoe on the other foot, and let a person know that you heard a rumor about him—that he gossips too much. This creates a powerful incentive for him to stop.

See These Chapters for Additional Strategies:
⇨ Chapter 3: **Make Anyone More Moral and Ethical**
⇨ Chapter 5: **Eliminate Prejudice in Anyone**
⇨ Chapter 9: **Give the Gift of Self-Esteem**

Chapter 17

Make Anybody More Open and Expressive

He doesn't share; he hardly even talks. He offers one-syllable responses and sometimes just grunts. The good news is that the ability to get such a person to open up to you is simply a matter of following a specific psychological strategy, as outlined in the following.

Technique 1: Be Smart

Suppose your brother is very closemouthed. To get him to open up, you must become the perfect sounding board. This means you should:

- talk about what is on his mind and what he is interested in.
- listen with your full attention.
- ask questions and follow-up questions.
- show excitement and genuine fascination.

Once you get him talking about what he is interested in, it will be much easier for you to steer conversations into another direction, to a topic that *you* want to talk about. But first let your brother practice being open in an area where he is comfortable. Encourage him to continue by being actively engaged in what he has to say. He will shut down immediately if he feels you are not listening to him and are bored by what he has to say.

Remember, no one wants to pour fine wine into a leaky milk carton. It makes people feel good to open up and express their feelings, but they have to believe that you will keep their confidences to yourself, not blab them to others. And no one wants to be judged negatively or to be talked about to others about how he feels.

EXAMPLE: *Paulette wants her boyfriend, Malik, to be more open about his feelings.*

When both of them are in a fairly good mood and have plenty of time, Paulette could open the conversation by asking to hear more about Malik's hobby, his thoughts on the political scene, and so on. "Tell me again your theory on the greenhouse effect? That is so interesting. Did you ever think about submitting it to a scientific digest? Really? . . ."

While this is not rocket science, we too often make the mistake of thinking that someone is nonexpressive when what is really going on is that he is not interested in us. Be interested in him, and you will help to widen the gates of communication. Listen to him with full and complete attention. Also, invite conversation when he is not preoccupied with something else. Once he is in the habit of sharing his thoughts by being mildly encouraged, he will begin to do so more naturally, more easily, and more often.

Technique 2: Anxiety Loves Company

A study by psychologist Stanley Schacter (1959) shows that a person seeks out company most when he is afraid or anxious about something. In this experiment Schacter had two groups of women come to his office laboratory. One group was greeted by a frightening man in a white lab coat who told them they would be given shocks in order to study the effect of electricity on the body. He added that the shocks, while painful, would cause no permanent damage.

The other group of women were met by a warm, smiling doctor who said the shocks would produce only a tingling, possibly pleasant, sensation. Both groups were then offered the opportunity to wait alone in a private room or in a larger room with others while the experiment was being set up. Of the thirty-two individuals in each group, about two-thirds of those in the high-anxiety group chose to wait with others, while most of those in the low-anxiety group chose to wait alone.

EXAMPLE: *Ursula wants her friend, Pam, to open up to her about her difficulties with her boyfriend.*

When Ursula's friend is waiting for the results of a test or to hear back about a job interview, she will be most motivated to seek out conversation and support. This is the ideal time for Ursula to engage her friend in conversation, as her friend will be more willing to open up.

Technique 3: Pull Back

It is rare that a person does not open up in *any* of his relationships. If he is closed, it is often the case that the other person helps to foster his behavior. This is because relationships seek their own equilibrium. By creating a space where the other person is not constantly in the listening mode, you allow for each of you to take on different roles and behaviors, thus moving him to be more talkative and you to listen more.

EXAMPLE: *You want your sister to discuss how she feels about your parents' divorce.*

If she's not talking enough, maybe you are talking too much. Try to limit what you say, but not in an angry way ("If you're not talking to me, I'm not going to talk to you"). Rather, be kind and courteous, but don't seek to elaborate on conversations about yourself and your interests.

Technique 4: You Looking at Me?

A study, commenced in 1927 by Harvard Business School researchers and named after the plant of the Western Electric Company, led to what became known as the Hawthorne effect. One aspect of the study was to determine if better lighting would lead to increased productivity. To everyone's surprise production increased when the lights were turned up *and* when they were turned down. What was going on? It turned out that the productivity was the result of the workers being pleased by the attention they received. The actual working conditions, whether they were favorable or unfavorable, didn't seem to make a difference.

A little girl who acts up for attention does not care whether she gets a positive response or a negative one. She just wants someone to care enough to do something. This is why parental experts tell us that this child needs private time with her parents to bond and grow; the last thing she needs is to be screamed at. The psychology here is to let your complaints about a person's lack of expression take a backseat to your investing yourself in the person and your relationship, whatever it is. Focus you efforts on being a good friend, parent, spouse, etc., and you may find that he naturally becomes more open and expressive.

EXAMPLE: *Mark wants to improve his communication with his daughter, Rebecca.*

Mark resists the temptation to chastise or criticize. Instead, he finds out what Rebecca is interested in, and learns about it. If she like poetry, he takes out a few poetry books from the library, and maybe goes with her to a poetry reading. By taking the time to invest himself in Rebecca's likes, Mark shows an interest in her as a person and not as a parent simply doing a job of raising a child. In any relationship, when you invest yourself in a person's life you become part of it, and that person's desire to open up is greatly enhanced.

Technique 5: The Bureau

A study was done with FBI trainees, who took part in a simulated abduction. Before the exercise, some of the trainees who were "hostages" for four days were told to concentrate on their feelings. Others were told to focus on the situation. The former group had a much greater need to talk about their feelings. It was concluded that in difficult circumstances those who focus on their emotions instead of the objective facts had a greater need to connect with, and to open up to, others (Strentz & Auerbach 1988).

EXAMPLE: *Winston wants his friend Nancy to open up about her feelings toward him.*

Whenever Nancy finds herself in a frustrating or difficult situation, Winston should pay particular attention. To get her to open up, he should ask questions about her feelings, and not facts. For instance, if she had a fight with a coworker, he should say such things as, "It must be so frustrating to deal with someone who doesn't care about your feelings," and "Are you more hurt or angry?" Such questions will get Nancy to open up much more than would questions about the facts of the argument, who said what to whom, and where the blame belongs.

Strategy Review

- Be the perfect sounding board. Ask questions, and show appreciation and genuine fascination in what a person has to say. This positive reinforcement will encourage him to continue opening up to you.
- When a person is afraid or anxious, he is more likely to seek out others. This is a prime time to engage the person, as he will be much more open and expressive than usual.
- If you want someone to talk more, you may need to talk less. Relationships seek their own equilibrium, and so he will naturally adopt more of the speaker part.
- Invest yourself in a person's life, and he will return the investment by expressing himself and being more open and communicative with you.
- In the mists or aftermath of any difficult situation, get the person to focus more on his feelings and less on the facts and he will open up to you infinitely more.

See These Chapters for Additional Strategies:
⮕ Chapter 8: **A Quick-Fix Pick-Me-Up**
⮕ Chapter 14: **Make Anyone More Assertive**
⮕ Chapter 18: **Turn Any Wallflower into a Social Butterfly**
⮕ Chapter 23: **Make Anyone More Respectful**

Turn Any Wallflower into a Social Butterfly

Bernice doesn't seek out conversation or friendship. She prefers to be by herself, and even if she is bored she will do anything but go out and meet friends. If you want to move Bernice from the corner of the room to the center of attention at a party, then use the psychological techniques in this chapter to get her onto the floor.

Technique 1: A Whole New World

Do you know someone who might engage in behaviors while on vacation that he would never dream of at home? And with little or no dissonance (internal conflict or guilt)? Research shows that heightened self-awareness increases one's need for consistency between attitude and behavior. Thus, when a person is in an unfamiliar place with no "reminders" of his life, the link between attitude and behavior is severed.

While logic might dictate that you want a person to be in comfortable surroundings in order to feel easier about socializing, often it is precisely the familiar that snaps him into his old patterns. New places and new surroundings help to facilitate new behavior.

And while sometimes just one experience can bring a person out of his shell for good, several experiences over a short period of time are most effective for changing the person's behavior in a more permanent way.

EXAMPLE: *Henry wants to help his brother-in-law, Amos, get rid of his party anxiety.*

Henry might take Amos on a trip away from his usual friends and influences. Or they could go to a party where they do not know anyone. Also effective is for Henry to have his brother-in-law dress a little differently than usual. As we've seen previously, appearance greatly affects attitude, and so a new look can help to facilitate a new behavior.

HOME FOR THE HOLIDAYS

Why is it that after ten minutes back home with the family, normal, happy, and healthy adults revert to the same old patterns and childish behavior they engaged in years ago? We snap back to familiar roles when we find ourselves triggered by the same dynamics—people and environment—that controlled us in childhood. But if you add one new person, a dinner guest perhaps, to the mix, or go to a new restaurant in a different city, the pattern is disrupted, and a person's character has a better shot at maintaining its integrity.

Technique 2: Improve Skills

Give your shy sister, for example, specific tools for improving her interpersonal skills. The ability to connect to others comes naturally to some, but most people need ways to pave the road to smooth conversation. Once your sister feels equipped to handle herself and builds up a track record of small successes, she will become more social and seek out friendships and situations to meet with others.

EXAMPLE: *You're bringing your shy wife, Keiko, to a business dinner with your boss.*

Practical social skills include expressing genuine interest in what someone is saying, responding positively, and asking questions: "What is it about skiing that you love so much? How did you become so involved in writing children's books? Have you always lived on the seashore?" Most of all, just let Keiko practice the "nod and listen," and people will find her fascinating because they will be talking about their most favorite subject—themselves.

Here are five key tricks Keiko can pull out of her conversational bag that will put her more at ease:

- Have her practice smiling and making eye contact.
- Get her used to asking questions about the other person.
- Arm her with one short, funny story or joke.
- Encourage her to use the other person's name when speaking.
- When appropriate, have her say something harmlessly flattering, such as: "What a great tie . . . Your cooking is delicious . . . You sure do know a lot about movies (or country music or books)."

Just knowing that Keiko has ammunition to counter that uncomfortable silence or awkward moment she so fears will help to put her at ease.

Technique 3: An Engaging Outlet

One of the easiest and most powerful ways to get someone to be more sociable is to get him involved in doing something he enjoys. Any hobby or sport where he is with those of a like mind with like interests will help bring him out of his shell. When he is with others who are similar to him, and doing what he enjoys, his inner self will be less inhibited. This also helps the person to make friends and enjoy special relationships.

When we excel at something, we are happy for others to be impressed by us. Therefore, even though you are dealing with someone who is not sociable, encourage the shy person to attend get-togethers that you arrange. Start with one other person, and then increase the number of attendees over time. In this way he will feel more comfortable, because he is the insider who has been there the longest. And with each new person's nervousness at being the "new guy," he will continue to grow in confidence by showing them the ropes.

EXAMPLE: *A mother wants her young daughter, Justine, to make more friends.*

If Justine has an interest in music, the mother can have her join a band or start a little music group with other kids. After a while Justine might even play music publicly with other kids. Whatever Justine enjoys—cooking, sports, writing, painting, etc.—the mother should enroll her in a group with others of a similar age and same sex who enjoy the same thing.

Technique 4: Center of Attention

How do you get an introvert out of his shell? Make him the center of attention. This is done by putting him in a situation—a contest or training session—in which he is the most competent. You can even make him a trainer himself. People will naturally seek him out, and he will feel good about it because he knows he will shine. If the person does not excel at anything, then you can put him with those who are younger or in some way disadvantaged so that he can be the most competent and capable person in the group.

Most of the factors that contribute to either shyness or introversion are muted by putting the person in a situation where he is the most capable. He will gain confidence, without performance anxiety, and he is guaranteed to receive constant reinforcement and positive feedback.

EXAMPLE: *Miguel wants his young son, Jason, to be more outgoing and sociable.*

Let's say Jason is a great archer. Miguel could arrange for other children, less skilled than Jason, to be part of an archery class, and his son can either be an instructor or a student. The other kids will naturally give him attention and praise, and he will feel good about being the center of attention. If Jason is good at math, climbing, computers, etc., then by surrounding him with those less skilled, Miguel will move him naturally to a more extroverted state.

Strategy Review

- If you are able to use leverage, then have the person visit or live in a new place. When a person is outside of his usual environment, he is able to more easily go outside his shell.
- Work with a shy person on improving communication skills. The better we are at something like socializing, the more likely we are to engage in opportunities to connect with others.

- An easy, yet powerful, technique is to have a person engage in whatever he enjoys doing, with others who share his interest. His personality will flourish under these conditions.
- By creating an atmosphere whereby a person is the most capable and proficient of all those in the group, he will gain confidence as the center of attention and influence.

See These Chapters for Additional Strategies:

➪ Chapter 9: **Give the Gift of Self-Esteem**
➪ Chapter 15: **Turn a Lazy Bum into an Ambitious Go-Getter**

Chapter 19

Change a Stingy Person into a Generous One

When the check comes, Mr. Cheapskate's arms are too short and his pockets too long. He is the last one to offer to pay for anything, and whatever he buys is always the cheapest thing he can lay his hands on. If you have had enough, then use these psychological techniques to turn that miserly cheapskate into a philanthropist.

Technique 1: Stop Begging, and Empower

When we are entirely in control of a situation, we usually feel a greater sense of responsibility. Giving Mr. Cheapskate complete autonomy over how he spends money may help to change his attitude toward it.

Psychologically speaking, the more you berate his behavior, the further you define his self-image as someone who is cheap. He has no real motivation to change. If he knows he is going to hear you say, "Well, what do you know? Mr. Cheapskate finally does something nice!" when he does perform an act of generosity, his motivation level will be quite low.

You may unwittingly be forcing him into the role of miser. He plays his part well because you play yours. Why not try pulling back and putting him, for a trial period, in complete control? You may find that he rebounds to a point where he doesn't have to be the "bad guy," and so he becomes looser with the purse strings.

EXAMPLE: *A woman's husband makes her account for every penny she spends, and she wants him to more generous.*

The woman would say something like, "Honey, I want you to know that I'm sorry for having badgered you all these years about how you spend our money. The truth is, if it weren't for your fiscal responsibility, we'd have a lot less to live on now. Of course, I do regret a bit not buying one or two silly things along the way, but you are so thoughtful in every other way. So I am not going to cajole you anymore. If something makes sense for us to buy, you decide, and that's fine with me."

Technique 2: Not Business as Usual

Suppose you find yourself twenty-five cents short for the bus. If you were to ask a stranger to help, do you think you would be better off asking for a quarter, thirty-seven cents, or some spare change? According to a research study, you're more likely to get results if you ask for thirty-seven cents. Why? Because it makes people think! This study showed that almost twice as many people contributed when asked for this odd amount than when asked for twenty-five cents (Santos et al. 1991).

Why wouldn't people do the easier thing—give a quarter instead of a quarter, dime, and two pennies? It seems that asking for thirty-seven cents got people to more carefully consider the request. If money was the only factor, then beggars and panhandlers would get a coin or two from everyone they asked—but they do not. The objective is to get the person to hear your request and give it thought. Asking for something routine and ordinary makes the request easy to dismiss.

When a person is forced to more closely consider a request, as one is forced to do with such an odd amount, it makes him more inclined to help. He cannot simply say no and go about his day. Instead he sees the person looking for bus fare as a human being with a specific need, not just someone mindlessly asking for something.

When you want a person to be more generous, you have to be sure he does not dismiss the request without giving you and your needs full consideration. Additionally, asking for an odd amount shows that you understand the value of money, as you are asking only for what you need, not rounding it off for the sake of convenience.

EXAMPLE: *A fundraiser is calling on Mr. Tightwad to donate money toward a new medical building.*

If the fundraiser merely asks for a donation or for a round number such as a hundred dollars, the request can be easily dismissed. Instead he says, "Mr. T., we'd like you to contribute $104 to the new building." Now Mr. T.'s curiosity is piqued, and he will be more inclined to say, "Why do you need, $104?" instead of "No." Now actively engaged, the fundraiser has the opportunity to continue to sell the idea.

Technique 3: A Dose of Perspective

Have you ever driven by a bad traffic accident and noticed that the people you're in the car with suddenly become nicer to one another?

There's a sort of quiet kindness that permeates the air. Or have you ever been to visit a friend at the hospital, and the second you walk out of the lobby doors you look around and see the world just a little bit differently? You feel a mix of relief, sadness, and optimism. You feel happy to be alive and grateful for what you have. These situations give us a healthy dose of perspective. That is why the best time to solicit a donation, or to get someone to help you, is when the person has recently had such an experience. He will be more inclined to give as he seeks to attach himself to something that is more real and permanent.

EXAMPLE: *Any time you get a gift from your father, it is always small and frivolous.*

Take your father to visit an aging or sick friend or relative. Let him see that life does have an end and the purpose of it is not to die with the most money. This will help him connect with the idea that it is only what we do for others, not what we have, that defines us and makes us who we are.

Technique 4: Advance, Then Retreat

In Technique 4 you ask someone for a much larger request than he is likely to agree to. And then after he refuses, you ask for something smaller—the thing you really want. Cialdini et al. (1975) asked college students on the street if they would be willing to volunteer to be an unpaid counselor for juvenile delinquents two hours a week for a two-year period. No one said yes. But then, before the subjects walked away, they were asked if they would agree to take these same kids on a two-hour trip to the zoo. Fifty percent of the students said yes. However, when students were asked about chaperoning the zoo trip without first being asked the larger request, only seventeen percent agreed.

The psychology here is threefold: (1) after the other person makes a concession, we feel the need to reciprocate; (2) we don't want to be perceived as unyielding and unreasonable; and (3) we want to think of ourselves as good, and so we seek to get rid of that "bad" taste of not helping by doing something easier and less demanding.

EXAMPLE: *Gary wants his father-in-law, Mr. Smith, to invest thirty thousand dollars in his new company.*

After Gary explains the idea, he says to his father-in-law, "So to really get this off the ground, we need about two hundred thousand dollars." After Gary picks his in-law up off the floor, Smith responds, "That's too much money." Gary then pauses and says something like, "Well, okay. I can get most of it from a small business loan and the rest from savings. Can you put in thirty thousand?" Now Smith is relieved and is internally motivated to help Gary out in some way.

Strategy Review

- Empower a cheapskate to make all of the decisions. In a short time his attitude toward money should soften, and without you pushing, he will stop pulling back.
- Don't have your request be business as usual. Ask for what you want in a way that gets a person to think about the request, instead of easily dismissing it.
- Remind a person of the real value of life by shifting his perspective. Take him to visit a sick or aging friend to put him in touch with what matters and what is important.

- If you first ask for a much larger request and then retreat to a smaller one, people are more likely to agree to give you at least some of what you want.

See These Chapters for Additional Strategies:

⇨ Chapter 8: **A Quick-Fix Pick-Me-Up**
⇨ Chapter 9: **Give the Gift of Self-Esteem**
⇨ Chapter 23: **Make Anyone More Respectful**

Chapter 20

Help Anyone to Feel Less Guilty about Anything

Guilt is a negative force that weighs us down, causing us to engage in unconsciously motivated, self-destructive behavior. We have all done things in life that we are not proud of, things we would rather undo. But guilt is useless, destructive, and eats away at us—*unless* it creates the impetus for action. In that case what we really have is regret.

Using the following four-step process, you can help a guilty person transform his negative feelings into positive emotions, and turn guilt into regret and regret into action.

- STEP 1: STOP THE BEHAVIOR. If a person is still engaging in the behavior that he feels bad about, he must stop it. If he cannot stop himself instantly, then have him make a plan that allows for the elimination of this behavior over a period of time—and then stick to it. In this way he will be moving toward his objective and will feel better about himself.

- STEP 2: TRY TO MAKE AMENDS. If he has wronged a person, have him make amends by using the techniques in Chapters 24 and 25. If he has done something that cannot be corrected or made better (or that does not involve anyone else), then have him speak aloud of his regret. As discussed in a previous chapter, the power of verbalization makes our commitment more real than if we were merely to think it to ourselves.

- STEP 3: SOLIDIFY IN THE REAL WORLD. How can you be sure that the behavior will not happen again? In addition to either stopping the behavior or making a plan to curtail it, he needs to put into action a plan that will help him keep the situation from recurring—in other words, something that will make it less easy for him to repeat the transgression. In this way he is saying to himself and to the rest of the world that he is a changed person, a new person who is doing whatever it takes to make sure that the "improved him" takes hold.

- STEP 4: A STEPPING STONE FOR GOOD. Take whatever he's done, and see how he can turn the experience into something positive. Regardless of what it is, use it as an impetus to do something good for someone else. If this is not possible, then have him make a commitment unrelated to the mistake to do something productive—an act that he would otherwise not undertake.

These four simple steps have a powerful ability to transform someone who is racked with guilt, and to help him to release it, feel good, and move forward in life. We are all human, and human beings make mistakes. Life is not about being perfect, but about what we do when we discover that we have acted wrongly. This is what defines us: how we move forward to make right when we have done wrong.

EXAMPLE: *A therapist has a client, Geoffrey, who feels bad about how he treated his parents.*

If the relationship is still ongoing, then the therapist should suggest specific things Geoffrey can do to demonstrate his affection and gratitude toward his parents. He should try to make amends as well by apologizing to his parents, being specific about what he has done.

Furthermore, Geoffrey should be encouraged to eliminate whatever catalyst led to his misdeeds. For instance, if he has a behavioral problem after he drinks, than he should join a program such as AA; if he has a problem with anger, he should attend an anger management class.

If the relationship still exists, Geoffrey should make a goal of speaking with, or visiting, his parents a set number of times each month. And if the relationship is nonexistent, the therapist should encourage Geoffrey to do something positive in the merit of his new outlook. For example, this could include volunteering in a senior citizens' residence, or working with families that have a rift or estrangement between them.

See These Chapters for Additional Strategies:
⇨ Chapter   9: **Give the Gift of Self-Esteem**
⇨ Chapter 24: **Make Anyone More Apologetic**
⇨ Chapter 25: **Erase the Anger and Make Anyone More Forgiving**

How to Change Anyone's Attitude and Behavior

Use the Power of Psychology to Rid Anyone of a Negative Attitude About Anything and Eliminate Any Unwanted Behavior. Whether it is Your Patient, Child, Friend, or Spouse, Help Someone Who Doesn't Want to, or Thinks He doesn't Need to, Change — Fast and for Good.

Foolishly held consistency is the hobgoblin of little minds.

— RALPH WALDO EMERSON

Chapter 21

Infuse Anyone with an Unwavering Sense of Responsibility

Roger lives life like someone else is pulling the strings. He blames everyone but himself for his problems—from the world to his mother. He tells you he will help with something, and then he is nowhere to be found. If you have had enough of his irresponsibility, then apply the following psychological techniques to turn any aimless do-little into a reliable and responsible person.

Technique 1: Lead by Example—or Not

When it comes to children, spouses, coworkers, and others with whom you spend considerable time, the best way to have them behave more responsibly is to lead by example. Your conduct has a greater influence over other people than you might imagine. How many parents teach their children not to lie, but inform their spouse that they are not home if so-and-so calls? Those around you pay close attention to what you do. So let them learn from you.

Now, for some people you have to do the exact opposite. Roger, for example, behaves irresponsibly because he knows you will always be there to pick up the pieces or take up the slack. So start with the first approach, and if you do not get too far with leading by example then switch to this tactic, and you will find he takes on the role of the responsible one as you move away from it.

Again, first demonstrate proper conduct through your own actions. Even when something is difficult to do, you nonetheless do it. You also do what is asked of you to the best of your ability, regardless of what it is, and wherever possible you strive to exceed expectations. Alas, switch to plan B, and responsibly remove yourself from the role of caretaker and fixer, and you will find that he, as a matter of self-preservation, will pick up the slack.

EXAMPLE: *A mother wants her children to take better care of their toys.*

The mother should be diligent in taking care of her own belongings. Everything she does in caring for her jewelry, plants, furniture, car, and so on, should be clearly demonstrated for the children to witness. If this doesn't work, then in a very responsible way she should not pick up the children's toys or bring them indoors when it begins to rain. (With children, adults need to remember that they are still ultimately responsible, and they should never hold children accountable for anything that is beyond their understanding.)

Technique 2: Rise to the Occasion

Develop a sense of obligation: it's important to let this person know that he is the only one who can help with a particular objective. And because of his help, you are going to—in some way—alter what you were going to do. He also needs to see that the withdrawal of his offer will cause you hardship. If he reneges and there are no repercussions, then he will see that things are no worse off for you than before he agreed to help. Therefore, he will not feel as if he is letting you down, because you haven't suffered a loss.

This works well for the short term, and it also lays the groundwork to turn him into someone who is more responsible and who follows through on his commitments.

EXAMPLE: *Peter, an office worker, wants his colleague Pamela to follow through on a promise to help him.*

Peter says, "Pamela, I just want you to know that I so appreciate your agreeing to help that I am canceling other appointments and moving my schedule around to work with yours." He then mentions any consequences he might suffer if she doesn't come through. And if possible, he involves her ego, making it known that what he needs from her cannot be done by anyone else—not simply because he cannot find someone else, but because she is the best to deal with it. "I'm in hot water if this doesn't get done, so I'm thrilled that I can count on you, because you know this system better than anyone."

Technique 3: I Believe You Will

There is a classic story about a teacher in one of the worst school districts in New Jersey, where one particular class of kids constantly got Cs, Ds, and Fs. They were disruptive and unruly—the worst. Finally, a new teacher came in from another school district, and she took over the class. Inside of one semester, the students' grades improved to Bs, Cs, and Ds. By the second semester, the entire class had an overall B-minus average, something that had never happened before.

The school district honored the teacher with a Teacher of the

Year award. At the ceremony, the superintendent said to her, "You took the most unruly group of kids, one that no one could come near helping. You made them a class that wanted to learn, wanted to become better, wanted to get good grades, were never absent, and were not disruptive. How did you do it?"

The teacher said, "I don't understand what you're talking about. These kids all had above average IQs."

The superintendent of the school said, "Ma'am, if it must be told, they really all have below-average IQs."

The teacher said, "No, look here." And she whipped out a paper and said, "I looked at these numbers before the class started: 125, 130, 140, and 118. I mean, these are some high IQs. When I saw these IQs, I went in there every single day, and I trained them and taught them and lectured them like they were smart people. If they asked a question, I said, 'That's a great question; only smart people ask those kinds of questions.' I treated them like they were real smart people, and they did well."

The superintendent said, "Ma'am, those aren't their IQs. Those are their locker numbers."

This teacher didn't talk to those kids as though they were idiots. Instead, she spoke to them as if they were bright people. If someone asked a question, instead of saying, "That's a stupid question," as teachers had done before, she responded, "That's a great question. You're a smart person."

Every single thing you hear, particularly when you are young and especially from a teacher, you value as gospel. And if a teacher says you're dumb, guess what? You think you're dumb. But a teacher says, "That's a good question; that's a bright question," guess what? You become smarter because of it.

Studies done across a broad spectrum of fields, from military training to the workplace to home care, have drawn a unanimous conclusion, one that is outstanding in its implications: when we have knowledge that a person believes in us, that we are capable, we work harder to meet his or her expectations.

Whether you are dealing with children, employees, or the gas station attendant, your expectation of performance will increase the actual performance.

BOYS AND GIRLS

Expectation of performance extends to a wide range of areas. In a study where female college students stated that they believed men were better at math than women, the women did more than three times as poorly as men on the same test. However, women who believe that there are no real differences in math aptitude between men and women scored just about as well (Spencer & Steele 1996). Our own expectations, as well as those that others have for us, greatly affect our actual performance.

The power of expectation is enormous. Indeed, your confidence in a person and your expectation that he will be more responsible will help boost his own confidence and his expectation of himself. He will not want to let you down, and when you see his true potential, he will in time come to see it in himself.

EXAMPLE: *A teacher wants Martin, a problem student, to be more diligent in his studies.*

In the classroom the teacher responds to Martin as if he were a genius in the rough. Therefore, any answer Martin gives that seems wrong might be met with, "What an interesting approach" or "I don't think that's right; think about it and it will come to you, I know." Outside the classroom the teacher would ask about Martin's plans when he gets older, encouraging him to fulfill his latent potential.

Technique 4: The Fox and the Henhouse

When someone slacks off, he very quickly, sometimes even unconsciously, justifies his behavior. However, when a person becomes responsible for getting others to do the very thing he has been lax about, he is more motivated to be successful. He must now reconcile the discrepancy between his own actions and his attitude toward others for violating the same behavior. To release the burden of this internal conflict, he has to either fail miserably at his job or change his behavior. If the incentive to perform well at his job is high enough, then his own behavior will shift to fall in line with his new role.

EXAMPLE: *A sales manager wants her salesman, Devon, to be more responsible.*

Suppose Devon falls short on his quota of sales calls and rarely, if ever, properly fills out his paperwork. The manager can make Devon responsible for implementing a program for making sure that all salespeople meet their quotas, and put him in charge of computerizing a new paperwork system. Now Devon will become a model of responsibility, because in order for him to be successful he must become more responsible.

Strategy Review

- Your conduct has a greater influence over other people than you might imagine. Act responsibly yourself, and watch those around you fall in line.

- Invoke a person's ego and conscience by having him commit to helping you with something that only he can best do.
- Expect the best, and let the person know it. We are apt to live up to the expectations others have for us—for better or worse.
- Put the person in charge of the very thing that he slacks off with. This creates a powerful psychological force that moves him into responsible action.

See These Chapters for Additional Strategies:

Chapter 22

Bring Out the Romantic Side in Anyone

"My husband is about as romantic as a rock. He rarely does anything sweet, and I have to beg him to do the little that he does." If you have had enough and want to turn a cold fish into Mr. or Mrs. Romantic, now you can.

Technique 1: Adopt-a-Persona

Have you ever met someone who in one situation was one way, and in another completely different? As though he had two personalities? There are many actors who are painfully shy offstage, and who cannot sit for an interview without sweating and stumbling over every word. Yet these same people can go onstage in front of thousands and perform calmly and flawlessly. How do they do it? They are just playing a role. It is not them onstage, but a character who for a while shares the same body. This is a great technique to get someone used to being, feeling, and doing romantic things.

EXAMPLE: *Ned wants his wife, Laura, to be more romantic.*

Ned asks Laura to imagine herself as someone else, and then to act as her. Perhaps they could watch a romantic movie, and then Laura could play the role of the actress. They could use props for atmosphere, and if Laura is willing, she could spend time rehearsing her "part."

Do not underestimate the effectiveness of the psychology here. We all have multiple roles in life. A woman may be a wife, mother, daughter, sister, professional, friend, and so on. And with each role we think, speak, and behave differently. So here we expand a person's repertoire to include a new role.

Technique 2: Emotional Nourishment

A person behaves with you, to a large extent, based on how you make him feel about himself. If you want someone to be more romantic, then you have to give him the capacity to give you what you need. It makes us feel good to give, but we need the emotional fuel to do so. If your spouse is not giving you the romance you want, did you ever ask yourself, *Am I giving him what he needs?*

It is no surprise that men and women are different and require different "feedings." What may be news, however, is that through simple actions you can make a big impact on your spouse's romantic expressions. Focus on the following. Men are ego-oriented, so a woman should be sure to tell him how smart he is, and how capable and fantastic she thinks he is. Women, on the other hand, are fed more through emotions: affection, interest, words of love, appreciation. If a man feeds his wife emotionally, she will have the fuel and desire to become closer and more romantic.

EXAMPLE: *Dorothy wants her husband, James, to be more attentive and loving.*

Outside the bedroom, Dorothy should feed James's ego. At least a few times a day she should seek out his opinion, compliment him on something he has done, and tell him how much she respects the way he handles himself in certain situations. For example, she could say, "Dear, I want to get your opinion on something. Do you think my father should invest in XYZ stock now, or hold off? . . . You're so good with Suzanne; I know how difficult she can be, but you just never lose you calm. You're great." These are little things, but they can make a colossal difference.

Technique 3: Tell and Sell

We must make sure that our spouse knows what we want. It is often the case that your partner is ready, willing, and able to do what you want, but has zero idea what that something is. Make sure you are clear in relaying your wishes. When it comes to romance, it is all too easy, for example, for a wife to assume that her husband knows what she likes and wants—but this may not be so. Once he knows, she should encourage him with positive feedback so he will become increasingly eager to please her.

EXAMPLE: *Larita wants her husband, Bob, to leave her little notes and poems, and to surprise her with romantic gestures.*

Larita should tell Bob exactly what she would like him to do. For instance, if she wants him to write her love notes, or to take her out to dinner once a week, she should let him know that this is important to her. Larita should give positive reinforcement and compliments every step of the way. If Bob's not doing something she would like, perhaps he is fearful of not meeting her expectations. If she does this for a short time, he will pounce on any opportunity to be more romantic.

Technique 4: A Whole New You

Sometime in order to change another person, we have to change ourselves. If you want your partner to be more romantic, try offering a different "bait." Without getting into a lengthy discussion on individual tastes and likes, we can say that human beings, as a function of human nature, enjoy new things. So you may want to offer your partner something new in you.

EXAMPLE: *Alexandra wants her husband to be more interested and excited by her.*

Alexandra can accomplish this in a variety of ways, from the clothes she wears to how she styles her hair, from how she acts to what she says. By shaking up her husband's perception of her, she will change how he sees her, which subsequently will change how he responds.

Technique 5: A World Away

As mentioned in Technique 1, most of us find ourselves in a variety of roles. This can be a hindrance, however. If your husband "sees" you in a role that is not romantic, he may have a hard time shifting gears. In other words, while a woman may be a terrific mother, her husband needs to see her as his wife in order to feel romantic. And while a husband may be a good and attentive son to his aging mother, his wife needs to perceive him in another way. Sometimes the romance loses its bloom because our perception of the other person is locked into an unromantic mode. The more time a couple spends together, the more intertwined these various roles become. In order to regain that spark, you need to isolate out your relationships with each other from all the roles you are involved in.

EXAMPLE: *Josh wants to reignite that spark he and his wife had when they were first married.*

Josh needs to be in "husband role" when he wants to be romantic. Conversations about the guys at work, garbage pickups, and allowable tax deductions may be interesting, but they will interfere with his romantic side coming through. He should keep the atmosphere and conversation focused on his wife and himself, so that she sees him clearly in the role that most inspires and excites her.

Strategy Review

- Have the person adopt a persona whereby he's just playing a role. In this way he can get used to behaving more romantically without feeling uncomfortable.
- If you feed a person emotionally, he or she will be more than willing to be more romantic.
- Be clear in what it is that you want, and give as much positive reinforcement as you can. This will make your partner more eager to do as you please, as he knows what to do and is getting great feedback from it.
- To increase your partner's "appetite," try offering a different "meal." If you shake up who you are, you will change how your partner perceives you.

- We all have different roles in life—some are romantic; most are not. Be sure to be in a romantic role in order to get your partner in the right mood.

See These Chapters for Additional Strategies:

⇨ Chapter 8: **A Quick-Fix Pick-Me-Up**
⇨ Chapter 9: **Give the Gift of Self-Esteem**
⇨ Chapter 23: **Make Anyone More Respectful**

Make Anyone More Respectful: Dramatically Change How Someone Treats You, Your Friends, and Your Family

Whether it is a friend, family member, or coworker, you can significantly transform how anyone treats you—and with very little effort on your part. The techniques in this chapter are elementary and simple to do, yet they lie at the foundation of every relationship.

And if you are dealing with someone who is either extremely selfish or not of such sound mind, it is not significant. These techniques give the person what he needs in order to act appropriately with you and those whom you care about.

Technique 1: Change Your Interactions

You can change dramatically how someone treats you by changing how you interact with him. When someone treats you poorly, it is usually because he does not feel good about himself. The solution is simple. If you give him what he needs emotionally, then he will treat you like pure gold. You can accomplish this by using any number of the following five keys.

EXAMPLE: *Your mother-in-law constantly belittles and embarrasses you.*

KEY 1: SHOW GENUINE ENTHUSIASM.

The power of this rule is astounding. If, upon seeing your mother-in-law, you walk over with a big smile and a genuine indication of pleasure for being with her, you will make her feel like a million dollars. She, in turn, will show vast appreciation for your making her feel so comfortable, welcome, and well-regarded. If your mother-in-law gets the feeling that your being around her is a chore, it will eat away at her self-esteem and the bond between you. When you speak with her, give her your full attention; do not read, watch TV, or have your focus divided in any way.

KEY 2: SHOW RESPECT.

Has someone you do not particularly like ever paid you a huge compliment? Or has such a person asked for your advice, presumably out of respect for your opinion? When this happens, we find ourselves forced to reevaluate our feelings toward these people and to adjust them to a more favorable reaction. If someone is a fool and asks us for advice, then that would mean that he does not know what he is doing in coming to us. We would rather simply adjust our opinion of him and conclude that maybe he is not such a bad guy after all.

This is known as *reciprocal affection.* We tend to admire, respect, and like someone once we are told that he has these same feelings for us.

KEY 3: BE SUPPORTIVE.

When your sister, for example, makes a mistake, let her know that it's something anyone could have done and that she shouldn't be so hard on herself. Do not be quick to criticize and condemn. She will only become defensive and argumentative. There is no merit or reward for being right or in proving that you are smarter than she is. You don't gain anything. There is, however, reward for showing compassion and support: a terrific relationship.

KEY 4: LET THE PERSON KNOW YOU APPRECIATE HIM.

It's amazing, but it seems that in all kinds of relationships, the only time we say something nice is when we've done something wrong. Be proactive from time to time. One nice word in the bank is worth a hundred after the fact.

KEY 5: ALLOW THE PERSON TO GIVE TO YOU.

We often think that people will like us if we do nice things for them, but the reality is that a person actually likes you more after he does something *for you*. There are several reasons for this: (1) Whenever we invest time, energy, and attention in anything—in this case a person— we feel closer and more attached. (2) When someone allows us to give, we feel better about ourselves, as giving reinforces the feeling that we are in control and independent. (3) And finally, doing for another engages the psychological phenomenon of cognitive dissonance whereby we conclude, partly unconsciously, that we must have a favorable impression of him. Otherwise, we'd be going around doing things for people we don't like. We'd rather conclude that the person is worthy of our investment.

Technique 2: Train Him

A person will treat you the way you train him to. If you do not let him know that certain conduct is unacceptable, then he may say and do whatever he wishes. Oftentimes a person is testing the waters to see what he can get away with. And if you do not speak up for yourself, then you are in effect condoning his behavior. When he does something you consider to be inappropriate or disrespectful, you need to tell him. Of course, *how* you say it makes a big difference, as illustrated in the following.

EXAMPLE: *You want your colleague, Wilma, to stop being a verbal bully.*

In front of others, Wilma says that you are incompetent. Avoid the temptation to say anything right then and there, because then she will have to save face by defending herself. The next chance you get, in private say something like, "Wilma, I'm sure you didn't mean anything by it, but I want you to know that what you said was offensive." She will either apologize or defend herself. If she apologizes, say thank you, smile, and let her know you appreciate her apology.

If Wilma tries to defend herself, her rationale will probably be that either you're too sensitive, or she was just trying to help. Either way, don't argue. You simply say, "I'm sure your reason was good, but what you said was offensive to *me*." And that's the end of the conversation. You needn't tell her not to do it in the future. However, should Wilma do it again, have the same conversation in the same way. It won't take more than two or three talks for her to stop her disrespectful ways.

Technique 3: Outsmart Him

As we said, a person treats you poorly because he needs to. Whether it's a ten-year-old on the playground or a fifty-year-old at work, this person does not like himself, and so he takes it out on you. You have a few options. You can change how he feels about himself, change how he feels about you, or take away the feeling that he gets when he tries to bully you. Then, even though he still has the need, you no longer fill his craving. Using Technique 3, you will take away the feeling that he gets. It's fast, and it works. You do this by undercutting his power, as illustrated in the following examples.

EXAMPLE 1: *Jason wants Marvin, the lunchroom bully, to stop picking on him.*

The scene is always the same. The bully goes over to Jason when people are around, picks up his lunch, and pours out his milk. To change this scenario, when the bully comes over, Jason might take one of the following steps.

- He can say, "Look everyone, here comes Marvin, the bully. Watch how important he is; because he's bigger, he can pour my milk out. Wow!"
- When Marvin approaches, Jason can take his own milk and spill it out in front of Marvin.

EXAMPLE 2: *Alice is always teasing Shirley on the playground.*

Mean Alice comes by every day to make fun of Shirley in front of her friends. What Shirley should do is shift the power so she is the one in control. Shirley might say, "Okay, everyone be quiet and give Alice your full attention, because she doesn't get enough at home. Okay, go ahead, Alice. You can make fun of me now." Now Alice is getting permission to be mean. This really takes the wind out of her sails, and after a few such treatments she will no longer enjoy teasing Shirley.

While these illustrations deal with children, the psychology is easily and effectively applied to adult situations using much the same language.

Strategy Review

- Show enthusiasm when you are with a person, and he will, in turn, show vast appreciation for your making him feel so comfortable, welcome, and well-regarded.
- Show respect, because it is very hard to dislike someone who not only likes us but also respects us.
- When a person makes a mistake, let him know that it's something anyone could have done and that he shouldn't be so hard on himself.
- It's amazing, but it seems that in all kinds of relationships, the only time we say something nice is when we've done something wrong. One nice word in the bank is worth a hundred after the fact.
- We often think that people will like us if we do nice things for them, but a person actually likes you more after he does something *for you*.
- People treat us the way we train them to. If someone acts disrespectfully, let him know, in the kindest way possible, that the behavior was offensive.
- Bullies bully because it makes them feel powerful. If you undercut their power, then anytime they try to "get you," they wind up feeling less in control.

See These Chapters for Additional Strategies:
⇨ Chapter 8: **A Quick-Fix Pick-Me-Up**
⇨ Chapter 9: **Give the Gift of Self-Esteem**

Chapter 24

Make Anyone More Apologetic

Small stuff or big stuff, it really doesn't matter. Getting an apology out of a person is like pulling teeth. If this describes someone you know, then you can make great progress toward turning him into someone who more easily apologizes when he is in the wrong.

Technique 1: By All Means Necessary

Get the person in a great mood, excited and looking forward to something. Joy (which is the anticipation of a future event) will enhance his mood and so temporarily give him a feeling of greater self-esteem. This often gives you the extra emotional oomph that you may need. Note that this is not merely a short-term measure; the more he apologizes, the easier it will be for him to do so. What Technique 1 does is build him into the kind of person who is more readily able to say that he is sorry.

Research shows that a person may have a reluctance to apologize if he thinks it will harm his good feelings. Avoid this psychological

trap by conveying that the other person is eager to hear him out and
will not make a big to-do out if it. Simply explain that it will be quick
and painless, and then he can get back to the exciting project/plan/trip
you have chosen.

EXAMPLE: *Nancy wants her husband to apologize to her father.*

Nancy can choose any event or even make it a surprise, as long as it
is something that draws her husband's attention and puts him in a
good mood. "Dear, I got you tickets to the game tonight. And then
afterward we'll go to your favorite steakhouse for dinner." Then a few
moments later, she adds, "Do me a favor. I'll get my father on the
phone. Just say you're sorry, and give the phone back to me. It will
mean so much to him. You know how much he respects you."

Technique 2: A Wake-up Call

You want someone to see what in life is really important. To do this,
take him to a hospital, a nursing home, or even a funeral parlor. Many
people seem to connect on this spiritual level more than on the logical
or emotional level, and it is often highly effective. Seeing that life in
fact does have a deadline, we become more reflective. This works so
well for us because we are looking at everything, including people and
situations, with more kindness and empathy. And this change in our
outlook gives us the opportune time to patch things up.

EXAMPLE: *Jasmine's friend Emily refuses to apologize to a mutual
friend for insulting her, and Jasmine wants to make peace between them.*

Jasmine may take Emily to a rehabilitation center or a burn unit of a
hospital. There, they spend time visiting and speaking with people
and their relatives, or even simply observing. Then Jasmine moves

into action while the emotional pull is strongest. As they leave Jasmine gives Emily her cell phone and has Emily call their friend, or at least commit to doing so, right then and there.

Technique 3: Straight from the Heart

Unfortunately, there is no shortage of people who would give their life savings to have a five-minute conversation with someone who has died. This person who has suffered such a loss makes a compelling case because it very powerfully invokes our target person's emotions. And when he hears a heart-wrenching, moving story, he has a harder time dismissing the emotions that he had tried to keep bottled up.

EXAMPLE: *You want to get your friend Marcia to apologize to someone she's hurt.*

Ask someone who never had the chance to reconcile before it was too late to speak to her. Let Marcia feel the full weight of the guilt this person is suffering. The self-destructiveness caused by not being able to make things right can be a powerful motivator.

Technique 4: Reshuffling the Deck

When you want to make peace between two people, use any significant event in either of their lives as a pathway to peace. Whether it's a birth or a death, positive or negative, such an event causes the psychological deck to be reshuffled, and you will have a better chance at drawing a new hand. The event provides the perfect opportunity to get the communication ball rolling.

EXAMPLE: *You want your father to apologize to his childhood friend for an argument they had several years ago.*

Any action—a phone call, card, or gift, for instance, to acknowledge an illness, crisis, or award—is one of the simplest and most powerful ways to achieve reconciliation. It makes it easier for the other person to forgive at these times, because he realizes the futility of holding on to grudges and anger in the midst of the things that really matter in life.

Technique 5: Ideal Steps

Often people fear not the apology so much as they do putting ourselves on the line only to be rebuffed. So you want to make an apology as easy as possible. Have the person follow these five simple steps to hearing the words, "Apology accepted!"

EXAMPLE: *You want to get your friend Brian to apologize to someone he's hurt.*

- STEP 1 APOLOGIZE. Make sure Brian is sincere and direct and accepts a hundred percent of the blame and responsibility. Now is not the time for "who said what first." If Brian takes full blame, the other person will almost always move into a more neutral position and insist on taking partial blame.
- STEP 2 DILUTE THE IMPACT TO THE EGO. Brian must show the other person that his actions were not meant as disrespectful, even though they appeared to be so. He should remind the person how much he admires and respects him, and he should apologize specifically for both his actions and the lack of respect that they showed.

- STEP 3 SHOW REGRET. Brian should convey to the person that he feels bad about his actions, and he should assure him that they will not be repeated.
- STEP 4 DEMONSTRATE PAIN. The offended party should know that Brian is in pain, suffering from both the guilt of his actions and the loss of the relationship. Ideally, the person should explain to Brian what has changed in his life since the incident and how it has been difficult for him.
- STEP 5 ASK FOR FORGIVENESS. Brian needs to ask the person to forgive him. Psychologically, this puts the person in a position of power and paves the way to more easily accepting Brian's apology.

Finally, try to talk to the other person ahead of time, and prepare him to be more open and receptive to hearing Brian's apology. Some of the techniques in this chapter and the next will prove useful in doing this.

Technique 6: I Confess: I'm Guilty

Research shows that when a person is sad, he is more likely to blame himself for a serious conflict than he would if he were in a good mood. Those in a good mood, however, were more likely to assume the *other* person was at fault (Forgas 1994).

But here is where it gets tricky. While a sad person is more likely to accept blame, studies also show us that a person in a good mood is more likely to actually make an apology. Therefore, the strategy here is to first take the person to a sad movie, for example, or discuss sad news in the paper. Then bring up the subject of blame regarding this current conflict. You will likely get more acceptance of responsibility. Afterward, you can use Technique 1 to put him in a good mood before you encourage him to apologize.

EXAMPLE: *Your friend Brenda has never apologized to your mother for an argument they had some time ago.*

After watching a sad movie, gently bring up the subject of who was really at fault. "Brenda, I was thinking about the fight you had with my mom. How do you feel about what you said to her?" Once she agrees she is, at least in part, to blame, tell her how much it would mean for your mother to hear her say that. Then after a few moments, bring up some happy and exciting news. Suggest that Brenda give your mother a quick call, apologize, and then the two of you can get back to your good time.

Strategy Review

- Get a person in a great mood, excited and looking forward to something. This joy will enhance his mood, and temporarily give him a feeling of greater self-esteem, while providing you with some of the extra emotional *oomph* you may need.
- Take a person to the hospital or a funeral home, for example, to jolt him back into reality. You want them to see what in life is really important and what really matters.
- A person who is in a similar situation makes a compelling case, because not only does it engage the law of social proof, but it also invokes his emotions very powerfully.
- Use any significant event in life as a way to get someone to apologize. A birth, for example, provides the perfect opportunity to get the ball rolling and open the communication gateway.
- In order to facilitate a person's accepting an apology, the person who wants forgiveness should follow these steps: be

sincere and direct, dilute the impact to the ego, show regret, demonstrate pain, and ask for forgiveness.

• People in a sad mood are more likely to admit fault than
are their happier counterparts. So before you ask a person
to apologize, get him to accept blame when he is in a sad
mood.

See These Chapters for Additional Strategies:
⇨ Chapter   8: **A Quick-Fix Pick-Me-Up**
⇨ Chapter   9: **Give the Gift of Self-Esteem**
⇨ Chapter 25: **Erase the Anger and Make Anyone More Forgiving**

Chapter 25

Erase the Anger and Make Anyone More Forgiving

Someone does something to us and we get mad. But why? Why do we respond with anger? Anger is the illusion of control. We hold on to the anger because then we feel that we have control over the relationship. The person is now dependent on us to forgive. Anger is a defense mechanism to feeling vulnerable. Yet in the end, it is only an illusion, and it offers no real satisfaction or lasting psychological comfort.

If there is someone in your life who is holding on to a grudge, try the four psychological techniques that follow to get him to be more forgiving.

Technique 1: The Approach

Before you begin to work your psychological magic, make sure your approach is sound. Following are some guidelines for how and when to get a person in the ideal state to accept an apology.

- When you are in a good mood, things do not bother you as much as when you are already upset over something. When you are upset, even the slightest annoyance can get under your skin. But when you are in a good mood, you tend to be more open, receptive, and eager to mend fences. So do not bring up the subject of an apology unless the person is in a good mood.
- Let the angry person know that he is in complete control. He can leave the conversation whenever he wants. He will not be begged to stay. He does not have to commit to anything else. He does not have to agree to do anything other than listen. There will be no come-ons or anything to persuade him.
- The angry individual needs to understand how the other person is suffering. It helps to reestablish balance. It is important to convey to the angry one that his misdeeds and the ensuing loss of the relationship have caused his "enemy" real pain. If the angry person does not believe that the other really cares and is hurting, you will not be successful.
- The angry person must know that the other person not only feels great pain and regret, but has also taken steps to correct the behavior. This shows that he's changed. It's not enough for him to feel bad. He must also undergo a kind of transformation to demonstrate that he is different from what he was before.

EXAMPLE: *You want Dennis to forgive Owen for taking a swing at him in a bar.*

When Dennis is in a good mood, say something like, "Owen has something to say to you, and he wants to know if you'd be willing to speak with him. He said he just wants one minute of your time, and you can get up and walk out at any time. And just so you know, he's been suffering greatly ever since this happened, and he has given up drinking entirely. As a matter of fact, he refuses to set foot in another bar."

Technique 2: Nothing to Show for It

It is important to let Dennis know that Owen's actions produced no enjoyment, financial gain, or any other type of benefit. Owen needs to explain that not only was his behavior a mistake, but it also did not produce the anticipated benefits either. Remember, the key lies in restoring balance to the relationship, be it personal or professional.

If Owen had gained in some way, then he would have to "give back" more in order to set things right. If he can make an investment—for instance, emotionally or financially—and show effort without benefit or progress, so much the better in restoring balance.

EXAMPLE: *Irene "borrowed" her father's car without permission and then dented the fender.*

Irene needs to fix the car now, or begin to make payments to do so. She has to take as much responsibility as she can for her actions. In any way possible, she has to restore balance. This means giving up whatever she gained. For example, if she used the car to buy something, she should return it. Every effort must be made to put things as they were.

Technique 3: Good for You

Even from a selfish standpoint, it is good for us to let go of the negativity of the past. Relationships are at the cornerstone of our mental health, and those that have soured drain us emotionally, spiritually, and physically. Let a person know that whether or not he feels he is in the right, it's good for him to forgive. Many studies show conclusively that a person's overall emotional *and* physical health improves by the simple act of forgiving another. This is true whether the motivation was to ease the pain of the offender or simply to release ones own emotional burden.

It is the strong who can forgive, while the weak need to hold on to anger and bitterness to feed and soothe a fragile ego. As we discussed, anger makes us feel grounded, and it gives us the illusion that we are in control and powerful. But really it is the weak who need anger. It is, after all, a false sensation, and it only fuels our ego while leaving us deflated.

EXAMPLE: *A clergyman wants to help Jeanne forgive her father for abuse, even though he is dead.*

Clearly, nothing Jeanne does will affect the relationship. Therefore, the therapist has her simply say the words, "I forgive you," while thinking of her father. If she does this, her attitude will be transformed. You do not have to understand why someone did what he did in order to forgive the person. In truth, it often doesn't matter.

Whether the abuser was abused himself, suffered from mental illness, or was an alcoholic is almost beside the point. Jeanne forgives him, not for him, but *for her.* Because forgiveness does not excuse her father's behavior, it allows her to put the past where it belongs— behind her. Even if she does not believe the words as she says them, after repeating them sincerely fifty times a day, she will in time come to embrace the meaning, significance, and truth in what she is saying. Do not underestimate the value of this technique. Affirmations can be a powerful tool in changing how you feel.

Technique 4: A Little Magic

Misdirection, the main principle in most magic tricks, is the art of drawing the audience's attention to one place, while the magician, undetected, manipulates the situation.

We know how effective misdirection can be with children. Their unrelenting crying, screaming, and indignant railing is replaced with a whimper and then squeals of delight when a lollipop is introduced into the equation. Of course, adults require a bit more, but the psychology is the same. Have something that you can offer the person that will redirect his attention, and you will have an easier time convincing him to forgive.

When you first suggest the idea of forgiveness, offer an immediate incentive, something he will receive, perhaps immediately, that he can focus on. The relationship and age of those involved will best determine what you can offer.

EXAMPLE: *Xavier wants Jill to accept his apology.*

After following the guidelines in the previous chapter, Xavier would say, "Jill, I know you don't have to forgive me, but I'd like to give you these tickets to the show anyway. Think about it, and take your time; I understand." As soon as Jill accepts the tickets, Xavier will have greatly increased the chance of getting his apology accepted. In addition to appreciating the tickets and engaging the law of reciprocity, Jill is now thinking about the show and so doesn't feel so much anger.

Strategy Review

- It is critical, to introduce the idea in the right way. Do so when the person is in a good mood. Let him know that he is in complete control, and let him understand how the other is suffering.

- Let the person know that the actions of others produced no enjoyment, financial gain, or any type of benefit whatsoever. Remember, the key lies in restoring balance to the relationship, be it personal or professional.
- Relationships that have soured drain us emotionally, spiritually, and physically. Let the person know that whether or not he feels he is in the right, it's good for him emotionally to forgive.
- A person will more readily forgive if his attention is divided between his anger and something that he finds pleasurable. Redirect his focus, and you soften his stance.

See These Chapters for Additional Strategies:

⇨ Chapter 9: **Give the Gift of Self-Esteem**
⇨ Chapter 24: **Make Anyone More Apologetic**

Chapter 26

Make Anyone More Interested in Anything

You like the opera, and she likes ice hockey. She loves to go out all the time, and you like to stay at home. From working out, to being with family, to taking trips, you can make whatever it is you enjoy her pleasure too. If you would like to get anyone interested in the things you like, then the following psychological strategies are here to the rescue.

Technique 1: It's Just Like That

Think of something you dislike. Chances are you know very little about it. Conversely, we are often quite familiar with things that we enjoy. The more a person knows about something, the greater the likelihood that he will come to like it. If you have a hobby, you know that the more intricacies you discover, and the more distinctions and nuances you explore, the more enthralled you become.

Therefore, when you want to get someone interested in something—gardening, for instance—have him learn as much as possible about it. Note that the aspects he discovers in gardening should ideally share the qualities of something he already likes.

EXAMPLE: *Marge wants her boyfriend Frank to be more interested in the opera.*

Frank loves car racing but hates the opera. What he loves about car racing is that it is competitive, fast-moving, and dangerous. So Marge shows, as best she can, where some of these very same elements exist in opera — and Frank naturally becomes more of a fan.

For instance, Marge might make Frank aware that thousands of people can try out for the lead role; that hundreds of operas compete for the ability to even be seen; that many operas have death scenes; and more money is earned by top performers than by rock stars. Clearly there are fewer things further apart than racing and opera, but getting Frank to focus on the qualities and aspects that both pastimes share can significantly increase his attention and interest.

Technique 2: Then I Must Like It!

Fascinating research shows an interesting relationship between reward and behavior. One study found that people who were paid $100 to perform a task rated it as more difficult and stressful than did those being paid $25 to perform the same task under identical conditions. When a person is compensated for something, he often finds the task to be more difficult and less enjoyable. And as the size of the reward increases, his motivation and interest decline (Freedman et al. 1992).

When we choose to do something, if we are not paid or otherwise compensated, we are unconsciously driven to like it more — otherwise, why would we be doing it? We prefer not to think that we made a mistake in choosing do so.

Another important factor needs to be considered: this technique works only if the person chooses—from at least one other option—to engage in the behavior. If he is told he has to do something, then the reverse happens: he finds the task less enjoyable the less he is compensated. However, if he chooses it himself, then he has to justify his actions, so he unconsciously assumes he must like it more, and thus he is not doing it for the reward. The person who had no choice is just annoyed that he has to do this, and annoyed that either someone else is getting more money or he's not getting enough.

EXAMPLE: *A father wants his daughter to try new and different foods.*

The father can tell the girl that if she tries chicken for two nights in a row he will give her a cupcake for dessert on the first night. Now, with the reward long in her tummy, when the second night comes she will reluctantly eat the chicken, rationalizing that she likes it, as no additional reward will be forthcoming. Now while she did receive compensation for her behavior, the fact that it no longer benefits her gives most of the psychological wallop of no reward in the first place.

If the child is simply offered a reward—chicken, then a cupcake—she would accept that she is eating one to get the other. But if she has to eat chicken the second night without any reward, because she agreed to do so, she is forced to reconcile her feelings toward the chicken by unconsciously concluding that she likes it. Why else would she have agreed to eat it, with the taste of the cupcake long gone?

Technique 3: Make It as Easy as Possible

When it comes to doing something we like, we glance over the numerous details, but when it comes to things we don't enjoy, we dwell on every detail. So if you want someone to change, you're going to have to show him that it's simple and easy.

If you want to *encourage* a behavior—for example, working out—emphasize the speed and ease of what needs to be done. When you want to *discourage* a behavior, stretch out the number of steps into a long, boring, and arduous process. It's the same event, but depending upon how it's internalized, you'll generate a completely different attitude toward it.

EXAMPLE: *Angelica wants her husband to eat better and exercise more.*

Angelica sees that healthy foods like fruits and vegetables are cut up, washed, and ready to eat, and that workout clothes are clean and available. Whenever possible, Angelica should encourage her husband to work out, making statements such as, "Why don't you take a fast run around the high-school track?" and "Grab a quick twenty minutes in the morning, and then I'll just drop you off at work." While these phrases seem obvious, notice the difference in how someone can present the issue: "In the morning, instead of hitting the snooze bar four times, get your lazy self out of bed, and drag yourself into the gym to work off that hero you just ate." Not very motivating, is it?

Technique 4: Arousal Approach

Have you ever been so bored that you eagerly talk to the telemarketer who phones, even though you have no interest in what he is selling? Or have you been so utterly bored that you'd do anything to get out of the house, even take a ride with a friend while she did her errands?

The arousal approach to motivation states that a person tries to maintain a certain level of stimulation and activity. Similarly, the *drive-reduction model* states that if a person's activity levels become too high, he seeks to reduce them. But it also states that if a person's level of stimulation is too low, he will try to increase it by seeking out higher levels of stimulation through various activities. Thus, even the laziest people can become fed up with doing nothing. To maximize the effectiveness of Technique 4, we combine this psychology with a cognitive approach called *expectancy-value theory*. This essentially states that a person is more inclined to act if he believes that he will be successful in his efforts.

EXAMPLE: *Lawrence wants his grandson to learn more about the family business rather than wasting the summer.*

Lawrence waits until his grandson has very little to do, so that his desire to seek stimulation by doing something, anything, is piqued. Then Lawrence offers him an opportunity where the results are guaranteed. For instance, he might ask his grandson if he wants to work at the company next week for X number of dollars.

Because Lawrence asks when his grandson is inactive, the young man's response is more likely to be positive. If he is already engaged in activity, he may not be driven to increase his arousal. Furthermore, because Lawrence offers his grandson a specific reward instead of simply a commission or a "We'll see how you do," his grandson is even more inclined to agree.

Strategy Review

- Bring out elements of an activity you want a person to like, and show him how they are similar to something he already likes. He should then become similarly interested in this new idea.
- Studies show that if we do something, we will enjoy it more if we are *not* compensated for our behavior.

- Make it as easy as possible for a person to get into motion, and help to establish momentum.
- Combining two powerful theories of motivation, ask the person to comply when he is inactive, and then offer him a specific reward or benefit for his work.

See These Chapters for Additional Strategies:

Chapter 27

Stop Passive-Aggressive Behavior in Anyone

A woman is unable to confront conflicts head-on, so she indirectly "gets back" by causing harm or inconvenience in a seemingly innocent manner. If you've got someone in your life who is driving you crazy with passive-aggressive ways, then use the following techniques to get the person to confront and discuss instead of secretly seething and plotting.

Technique 1: Reverse, Reverse, Reverse Psychology

Ask for the person's advice on the very thing that he is making difficult for you. The psychology behind this technique is twofold. First, the person makes an investment, but he also wants his investment to pay off, and that can happen only if things go easy for you. If he makes life more difficult, the stress and turmoil may cause you to be ineffective—and his advice useless. We all want to be right, and so he will try to make things as easy as possible for you so that you can benefit from his "wisdom."

EXAMPLE: *Christina, an office manager, has a secretary, Della, who frequently misfiles things.*

Christina could ask Della to devise an improved system for filing. Once it is in place, the only way Della's system can be useful is if Christina does not spend her time trying to track down files. Therefore, Della will not only refrain from sabotage, but she will try to make things easier on Christina. The less time Christina spends looking for files, the more effective Della's system is.

WHEN THE SHOE IS ON THE OTHER FOOT

When something is bothering you, or another person's actions frustrate or annoy you, bring it up; don't let it fester and become more serious than it already is. Keeping feelings inside you is rarely good for a relationship or for you. Some guidelines for bringing up your concerns are: wait twenty-four hours before saying anything; approach him when you and he are not pressed for time or in a lousy mood; and couch what you have to say in nonaccusatory terms.

Technique 2: Make Life Easy

You want to make it as easy as possible for this person to talk about what is bothering her. She will not need to lash out in passive ways if she is able to air her grievance with you face-to-face. This, however, can be difficult for her. So put a plan into action that calls for her to tell you what is bothering her every day. In this way, she gets into the habit, in a nonthreatening way, of saying what is on her mind. If she is uncomfortable doing this, then ask her to simply write down her grievances. You will give thought to them, and with her permission, discuss them with her.

EXAMPLE: *Larry feels his wife, Lois, is behaving toward him in a passive-aggressive manner, and she is unwilling or unable to discuss with him what is bothering her.*

Larry invites (not tells) Lois to spend five minutes or longer, every day or any day, writing down anything that upsets her. Then she simply leaves him what she wrote. Larry does not argue about or criticize what she says, or try to defend himself. He simply thanks her for being so honest. In a short time Lois will have learned how to deal with upsetting issues. When neither Larry nor Lois is upset or feeling rushed, they should gently go over Lois's notes and discuss how they can address them.

Technique 3: I'll Show You

This technique makes it almost impossible for someone to act passive-aggressively toward you. First, you bring his behavior into the open by telling him that you are aware of what he has been doing. Next, you tell him that you know why he has been doing what he has and that you completely understand. The trick here is to make your reason something other than his being passive-aggressive.

EXAMPLE: *Horace has a friend, Wallace, who keeps making fun of him in public.*

Whether or not Horace has told his friend not to make fun of him doesn't matter. What he says now is, "Wallace, I understand why you make fun of me in front of everyone. It's because you think people will like me more than you, and so you say things to try to make yourself look better, and me worse. You can't help yourself, even if you want to."

Wallace, of course, denies the behavior, his motivation, or both.

Horace then follows up, saying, "I'm sorry; maybe I hit a nerve. Let's just drop it." Now any time a situation comes up, if Wallace makes fun of Horace, he will be admitting that Horace was right—and his ego won't let him do this.

Technique 4: The Take-Away

Whatever a person is doing to bother you, make it worse. By making conditions less favorable, you cause him to seek a truce and move to an emotional middle. This can done in two ways: you can either (1) make a declaration that unless he does his part you will no longer do yours, or (2) return the passive-aggressive favor and take action without saying anything. At some point it will force him to bring it up, and then you can have a more meaningful discussion because he will be suffering right along with you. Technique 4 should be used only when necessary, as it can create, for a short time, more friction than currently exists.

EXAMPLE: *Mary's husband, Bernard, never picks up after himself despite repeated requests.*

Mary should simply go on strike, and not do the laundry, dishes, or other housework that she normally does. Whatever Bernard ignores, she should ignore even more. Now, not only is he unable to engage in his passive-aggressive behavior, but he is worse off than he was before.

Technique 5: Backfire

Your brother inconveniences you because it gives him some type of emotional satisfaction. But if what he does always seems to backfire, and he ends up harming himself instead of you, he will quickly abandon his ways. Even though this process is largely unconscious, if your brother is unsuccessful in his attempts to inconvenience you, he will stop them as a matter of self-preservation.

EXAMPLE: *Madeline's coworker, Drake, does everything from eat Madeline's food to write down messages incorrectly.*

Whatever Drake does, Madeline makes it appear that it costs him, not her. For instance:

- Drake eats the salad Madeline had stored in the refrigerator. Madeline remarks, "Oh, I was going to return that salad; I found little bugs crawling in it."
- Drake "forgets" to tell Madeline about a sales meeting. Madeline says, "Oh, I was going to pitch your new idea. I guess it will have to wait."
- Drake spills coffee on Madeline's desk. She later says, "Oh, I had printed something out for you, but it's too wet to read. I'm sorry."
- Drake takes down a phone message incorrectly. Madeline says, "Oh, I'm swamped, so I thought we should split that sales call. Maybe we'll split another one."

Strategy Review

- Ask a person for help on something you are having trouble with. Now in order for him to be right and for his advice to be helpful, he will not only not sabotage you, but he will try to make things easier on you.
- Provide an emotionally safe way for a person to discuss what is bothering him, and in time you will retrain how he responds to negative situations.

- Bring a person's behavior out into the open, but assign a different reason for the behavior. Now any time he engages in it, he will be proving you right, which his ego won't let him do.
- By making things worse, you cause a person to seek a truce and come to the emotional middle.
- If whatever someone tries to do always seems to backfire, and he ends up harming himself instead of you, he will quickly abandon his ways.

See These Chapters for Additional Strategies:

⇨ Chapter   9: **Give the Gift of Self-Esteem**
⇨ Chapter 23: **Make Anyone More Respectful**
⇨ Chapter 25: **Change the Chronically Late Person**

Chapter 28

Change the Chronically Late Person

If it's one thing Evelyn is known for, it's always being late. She offers up one excuse after another, and sometimes doesn't even bother to do that. To change Evelyn, we'll apply a variety of psychological techniques.

Constant lateness is usually caused by one of two unconscious motivations. One is that a person like Evelyn needs to feel in control. Keeping others waiting puts her in a position of power, even if she's just late for a meeting or for dinner. However, if she is also late for things that only inconvenience *her*—if she rushes to catch a flight for vacation or never sees the beginning of a movie—then she may simply have "low time awareness." Some people just "feel" time differently. Evelyn may be unable to effectively judge and manage her time well, often ascribing a task to take a shorter time than she should, and getting caught up in endless distractions.

Regardless of the motivations, if you have had enough of waiting for someone, then try the following psychological techniques to get the person to be on time, every time.

Technique 1: Pay the Price

If the stakes are significant, you may be able to bring about a change in behavior. In Technique 1, you tell the person in advance that you will wait for a reasonable period of time and then you will leave without him. End of discussion. This is not to be done cruelly and coldly, but simply as a matter of necessity. You want to be on time. You would love for him to join you, but if he is unable to do so on an agreed-upon timetable, then you have to go without him.

EXAMPLE: *Whenever you have plans with your friend Vivian, she always keeps you waiting.*

You could say something like, "Vivian, we'd love to go to the movies with you, but we do not want to be late. We will come by your apartment at 5:35, and I will call you when we're in front of your building. If you are not downstairs by 5:40, we're going to leave." Now it's no longer a matter of inconveniencing *you*; rather, Vivian loses out on seeing the movie. Regardless of the unconscious motivations at work, if she *has* to be on time, she can be.

OFF-PEAK

Set a time that is unusual. Instead of 9:00, make it 8:57. Studies show that people are more likely to remember an unusual time, and will attach a greater importance to it. Additionally, when a meeting starts at a round time, such as 9:00 P.M., people often assume it really won't get started until 9:10 or so. But an odd time makes people think that the time the meeting starts has greater significance.

Technique 2: Relearning Time

A great way to eliminate chronic tardiness is to retrain the person in how to tell time. If he continually underestimates the time involved for particular tasks, you can show him—make him consciously aware—just how long things take. When someone says he will be over in five minutes, he's likely wrong. Get the person to be real and honest with time.

Retraining cannot be done overnight, but a person can indeed be retrained to be more "time aware." This technique is used with great effectiveness in time-management classes, where people see in black-and-white just how much time they waste and lose, allowing them to better plan their day.

EXAMPLE: *Your wife, Dawn, is never on time for anything and keeps you waiting for everything.*

Pick a day for Dawn to keep a time journal. Here she records how long things take her—from brushing her teeth to eating breakfast to getting home from work to going shopping. Then for the next few days she mentally tries to do an accounting of how long things that she is doing will take. Then after a few days she uses the journal again. She goes back and forth until she is able to "guess" with great accuracy how much time things take.

Technique 3: Let's Make a Deal

In this technique you appeal to the person's sensibilities. Clearly he has a hard time being on time. Therefore, pick your battles. Your need to be on time conflicts with his desire to not be bound by time. So really, why should you always get your way?

So make a deal: he has to be on time only for specific events, and at other times he is welcome to be late. Additionally, to prevent him from being late for the times he agrees to be punctual, attach a penalty to his tardiness regardless of how good his excuse is.

EXAMPLE: *Jerry's wife, Deborah, is always waiting for him.*

Deborah and Jerry each choose their priorities, and then they agree that he has to be on time for certain events. For instance, if it drives Deborah crazy to be rushing to the airport, then she picks the time that they leave. But for dinner with friends and movies, if Jerry is running late, that's okay. Now Deborah will not feel that Jerry does not respect her time, as this is what they both agreed to. However, if he makes it so they do not leave on time for the airport, as he had agreed, he has to do something for Deborah (which should be decided on in advance).

Technique 4: Psychological Anchors

Do you remember the lessons learned by Russian scientist Ivan Pavlov? In short, in the course of an experiment, he noticed that the dogs he was working with began to salivate whenever he walked into the room. They had learned that Pavlov's appearance meant that they would be fed. They salivated because they associated Pavlov with food *even without the presence of food.* This is what's called a *conditioned reflex,* and we have many examples of this in our own lives.

For instance, maybe the smell of cut grass brings back fond memories of your childhood. Or anytime you meet someone with a certain name, you have unpleasant feelings toward him because of a former experience with a person of the same name. These are all anchors. An anchor is an association or link between a specific

set of feelings or an emotional state and some unique stimulus—
an image, sound, name, or taste. When someone's current actions
are associated with unpleasant stimuli, he will begin to form an
unconscious link and get a negative feeling from what was once
pleasurable.

EXAMPLE: *You and your sister, Donna, work together, and she is always making you late for sales calls.*

When Donna is doing what you want her to—being on time—
anchor this behavior with a positive association. For example, bring
up pleasant news, remind her of something she is looking forward to,
give her an unrelated compliment, or thank her for making a special
effort. In a short time Donna will have such a positive association
with being on time that she will desire to do so on her own.

Strategy Review

- Change the stakes so the tardy person has more to lose
  than simply inconveniencing you. A person will make a
  greater effort to be on time if the consequences of being
  late are more severe.
- Some people simply do not have a natural understanding
  of how long things take. Help them to relearn the concept
  of time and time management.
- Just because you want to be on time and someone is late
  doesn't necessarily mean that he should always give in to
  you. Agree together, ahead of time, what he can be late for
  and what you want him on time for.
- Use the power of conditioning. When the person is doing
  what you want him to do—being on time—anchor this

behavior with a positive association. In a short time he will associate positive feelings with being on time.

See These Chapters for Additional Strategies:
⇨ Chapter 23: **Make Anyone More Respectful**
⇨ Chapter 25: **Stop Passive-Aggressive Behavior in Anyone**

Chapter 29

Change the Person Who Nags

You cannot take another minute of the incessant nagging and complaining about everything you do wrong or don't do at all. If you've had enough, then use the following psychological techniques to put an end to the nagging for good.

Technique 1: The Hostage Solution

This technique uses good old-fashioned common sense. Ask the person what his demands are, and then quietly and calmly discuss them. The worst time to argue is when the person is in the middle of nagging you. So, when you are both calm and relaxed, mutually agree upon what you will do—and what you do not wish to do. If it is reasonable, then agree to do it and follow through on your word. But if it is not something that you think you should be doing, then tell him why and have an open, honest discussion about it.

People who nag do so because they believe it is an effective way to accomplish what they want. However, if they see that it's more

effective to sit calmly and negotiate, then they will change their ways
when they have further requests.

EXAMPLE: *A husband and wife each think that the other nags too
much.*

When they are both relaxed and in a good mood, they should review
their duties and responsibilities. The rule is simple: *no one can amend
or change them for one week, until the next sit-down.* For instance,
if one of the husband's jobs is to take out the garbage, then the wife
is not permitted to remind him unless an agreed-upon time passes.
Then she can nag to her heart's content, because he should have at-
tended to the trash. However, if something is not on the list, she can
only request once that he do it, and after that, she cannot mention it.

Technique 2: Put It in Writing

Oftentimes it's not what a person wants you to do that is so bother-
some, but rather how he or she asks, and asks — in that irritating, annoying way. With Technique 2, we eliminate the annoyance of how
the message is communicated and instead focus on the request
itself.

When verbal communication comes with too much baggage,
switch to written requests. Additionally, writing it once and putting it
in plain sight offers the benefit of a constant reminder without the
annoyance factor.

EXAMPLE: *Frank and Hillary run a small family business, and
Hillary has been accused of being a nag.*

Anything that Hillary wants Frank to do should be written down on
a sheet of paper and placed on a bulletin board, along with the

requested time that it be done. If Frank cannot fulfill the request, then he responds in writing with his reason, and he makes a counteroffer about if or when he can get to it.

Technique 3: The Lightning Rod

The lightning rod, invented by Benjamin Franklin, provides a low-resistance path to the ground to carry dangerous electrical current away from the structure that the rod is attached to. It simply offers lightning a more appealing target. This technique uses a similar approach. If the nagger has something else to focus his attention on, something more significant, that will direct his attention so he will not be so concerned or consumed with nagging. This "rod" can be anything, positive or negative, in your life or in his, as illustrated in the following. Additionally, by making the focus of his attention something that is very important to him, you can make him almost completely ignore most everything else.

EXAMPLE: *A teenager, Margie, wants her father to stop nagging her.*

Margie needs a lightning rod to draw away her dad's attention. She might remind him of significant things going on in her life that cause her to be distracted or preoccupied. For instance, she might say, "I'm having a hard time with French class; my best friend is going through a hard time, so I want to be there for her; and I'm worried about getting into veterinary school, so I'm putting in extra hours of study." Margie's father, impressed by his daughter's wanting to help her friend and her efforts to work hard, might give her more leeway, letting the little things slide. People forget that others have lives and things going on in them. When we remind them of these things, it helps to refocus their attention, and they cut us some slack.

Technique 4: Uncovering the Mask

All nagging comes down to one thing: the person wants to be heard, to be recognized. For example, your mother does not complain about laundry on the floor, garbage that has to be taken out, or the way you drive, even though that is what it sounds like. Rather what she is asking is that you take her feelings and wishes seriously. She wants you to care that she cares. The solution, then, is to give her what she wants, so her neediness will not seep out as nagging.

The more you praise your mother, the more you might think she feels as if she is in a position to tell you how to conduct your life. But the opposite is true. The more you show appreciation and respect, the less her need to try to control your life. Technique 4 can be extremely effective in putting a grinding halt to a person's incessant nagging. Let's see how it works.

EXAMPLE: *Patty nags her younger sister, Peggy, about everything she does—and doesn't—do.*

Peggy tells Patty what she respects and appreciates about her and how much she admires what she has accomplished in her life—even if that's not much. Peggy might say, "I want you to know that I think the way you live your life is just tremendous. I am so proud of you. And I want you to know that even though I don't say it a lot, I really appreciate everything that you do for me."

Technique 5: Honesty . . . the Best Policy

Of course, you always have the option of being honest! For example, if you let your sister know the damage she is doing by nagging, you may be surprised at what happens. Nagging is not cute, or fun, or harmless. The truth is it damages relationships. Studies show that for married couples, nagging causes intimacy levels to drop, along with overall marital satisfaction. It is imperative that the nagger come up with a new way to communicate her wishes, or there may not be anyone left to nag. How you communicate this to her is very important, as illustrated in the following.

EXAMPLE: *Burt has had enough of his wife's nagging.*

Burt is specific about the damage the nagging is doing. "I want you to know that I love you, and I want us to spend the rest of our lives together. Now I know that I forget to do things, and I'm sorry for it. But we have to come up with another way of you reminding me, because it is simply making me not feel as close to you. It makes me resentful because I feel that you don't appreciate the things that I do. I know that this is my fault, so together let's see if we can't come up with a better way of communicating how things get done."

Technique 6: Avoiding the No-Win

In the eyes of someone who nags you, no matter what you do, you cannot win. If you don't do what the person is asking, you will get nagged more, and when you finally do it, there's little gratitude or appreciation. There is a sense of entitlement so that he feels he is owed this, and so even doing what he asks only makes things "even."

Therefore, you want to get the person away from this automatic sense of entitlement, because unless you work for someone, there is no rule that says you must do X and he must do Y. Responsibilities are shared, and in healthy relationships both partners contribute, not because they necessarily have to, but because they enjoy making the other person happy. Nagging removes this latter incentive, and so you end up with a tit-for-tat relationship.

EXAMPLE: *June's health-conscious boyfriend nags her to take her vitamins.*

June and her boyfriend make a rule that any time he asks June to take vitamins, he must say one positive thing beforehand and give his appreciation afterward: "June, I know you try to eat healthy foods. Just as a reminder, did you get a chance to take your vitamins today? I appreciate that you don't like them and that you take them just for me, so thank you." Now not only will June find it easier to hear her boyfriend's request, but his focus will be more on what she is doing right. Soon his nagging attitude will be replaced with gratitude.

Strategy Review

- Open the gateways of communication and have the nagger tell you precisely what he wants you to do, and how and when he would like you to do it.
- Avoid verbal confrontation altogether by having the nagger put all requests in writing. In this way any perceived negative tone and badgering are eliminated.
- Give the nagging person something else to focus on to draw his fire, so he will not be consumed with the little things that you do—or don't do—that bother him.
- Eliminate nagging at its source by giving the person what he needs: to be listened to, appreciated, and respected.
- Let the person know how the nagging is affecting your relationship so that he sees that he is losing more than he is gaining.

• If you get the nagger to switch his focus from what you are doing wrong to what you are doing right, then his nagging attitude will be replaced with gratitude.

See These Chapters for Additional Strategies:

⇨ Chapter 20: **Bring Out the Romantic Side in Anyone**
⇨ Chapter 21: **Make Anyone More Respectful**

Conclusion

Our chief want in life is somebody who will make us do what we can.

—RALPH WALDO EMERSON

The techniques in *How to Change Anybody* allow you to help those around you to live richer, more meaningful lives. In doing so, you will find the quality of your relationships with these people to be markedly improved.

As I said in the note to the reader at the beginning of the book, I keep in mind that any change you want someone to make needs to be in his best interests. This is because real, lasting change can come only through the person wanting to invest in himself and to be someone better. And this cannot happen if a change is not in the person's best long-term interest.

When you want to help someone become a better person, you will find that you have significant influence to help almost anyone to live a happier, more rewarding, and fulfilled life.

I wish you good relationships and a good life.

Bibliography

Allport, G. (1954). *The Nature of Prejudice*. Reading, MA: Addison-Wesley.

Asch, S. E. (1956). "Studies of independence and conformity: A minority of one against a unanimous majority." *Psychological Monographs*, 70.

Bandura, A., & Adams, N. E. (1977). "Analysis of self-efficacy theory of behavioral change." *Cognitive Therapy and Research*.

Bargh, J. A., Chen, M., & Burrows, L. (1996). "Automaticity of Social Behavior: Direct effects of trait constructs and stereotype activation on action." *Journal of Personality and Social Psychology*.

Cialdini, R. B., Vincent, J. E., Lewis, S. K., Catalan, J., Wheeler, D., & Darby, B. L. (1975). "Reciprocal concessions procedure for inducing compliance: The door-in-the-face technique." *Journal of Personality and Social Psychology*, 31, 206–215.

Dickerson, C. A., Thirbodeau, R., Aronson, E., & Miller, D. (1992). "Using cognitive dissonance to encourage water conservation." *Journal of Applied Social Psychology*, 22, 841–854.

Forgas, J. P. (1994). "Sad and guilty? Affective influences on attributions for simple and serious interpersonal conflict." *Journal of Personality and Social Psychology*, 66, 56–58.

Freedman, J. L., Cunningham, J. A., & Krismer, K. (1992). "Inferred values and the reverse-incentive effect in induced compliance." *Journal of Personality and Social Psychology*, 62, 357–368.

Freedman, J. L., and Fraser, S. C. (1966). "Compliance without pressure: The foot-in-the-door techniques." *Journal of Personality and Social Psychology*, 4.

Haney, C., Banks, C., & Zimbardo, P. (1973). "Interpersonal dynamics of simulated prison." *International Journal of Criminology and Penology*, 1, 69–97.

Santos, M., Leve, C., & Pratkanis, A. R. (August 1991). "Hey buddy, can you spare 17 cents? Mindfulness and persuasion." Paper presented at the annual meeting of the American Psychological Association, San Francisco.

Schacter, S. (1959). *The Psychology of Affiliation*. Stanford, California: University Press.

Spencer, S. J., & Steele, C. M. (1996). "Under suspicion of inability: Stereotype vulnerability and women's math performance." Unpublished manuscript, State University of New York at Buffalo.

Strentz., T., & Auerbach, S. M. (1988). "Adjustment to the stress of simulated capacity: Effects of emotion-focused versus problem-focused preparation on hostages differing in locus of control." *Journal of Personality and Social Psychology*, 55, 652–660.

ABOUT THE AUTHOR

DAVID J. LIEBERMAN, PH.D., whose books have been translated into sixteen languages, is an internationally renowned leader in the field of human behavior. He has appeared on hundreds of programs and is a frequent guest expert on national television and radio shows and networks such as *The Today Show*, CNN, *The View*, PBS, A&E, and *The Montel Williams Show*. Dr. Lieberman's techniques are used by the FBI, The Department of the Navy, Fortune 500 companies, and by governments and corporations in more than twenty-five countries. He lives in New Jersey.

D r. Lieberman offers a variety of special products and programs in the United States and throughout the world.

If you would like more information of any of the following please let us know, and a consultant will be happy to answer your questions and discuss how we can best serve your needs.

- ☐ Additional Products and Services
- ☐ One-on-One Phone Consultation
- ☐ In-Person Case Resolution
- ☐ Teleconference
- ☐ Video-Conference
- ☐ Customized In-House Training
- ☐ $\frac{1}{2}$ Day and Full Day Seminar
- ☐ Keynote Address

If you prefer, just ask to be added to our free mailing list today!

Email: DJLMedia@aol.com

Ask about our discount to registered nonprofit organizations, law enforcement, and governmental agencies and associations. These inquiries must be faxed on letterhead to 1-772-619-7828